Crusade Hymn Stories

Edited by
Cliff Barrows
With Hymn Studies and Personal Stories by
Billy Graham
and the Crusade Musicians

hope publishing company
5707 West Lake Street
Chicago, Illinois 60644

1967
Printed in U.S.A.

FOREWORD

One of the greatest contributions to the spiritual development of my life has come from the influence of sacred songs. As a young boy I learned to love our gospel songs and hymns, as well as the Bible, at my mother's knee.

And now, for over twenty years of Crusade evangelism, we of the Billy Graham team have witnessed the lasting appeal of these hymns and their power to unite the hearts of a congregation. Wherever Christians gather, the singing of these hymns and songs has been a vital and meaningful part of worship.

The stories behind the hymns have always fascinated me. I believe they provide some of our most inspiring devotional literature. CRUSADE HYMN STORIES brings together some of the favorites of Billy Graham, and of the members of our music staff. Of course, not all our favorites – or yours – are here, but there are enough to give you a hymn a week for a full year – to study, to memorize, to make your very own.

Try using them for your personal worship or for family devotions. We believe you will find that one of the purposes of this book – to help you sing "with the spirit and with the understanding also" – is being fulfilled.

In writing CRUSADE HYMN STORIES there has been an honest attempt to present the facts concerning the hymns, their origins, and their significance in the Billy Graham Crusades as we have known them. We do not claim that these are all the facts. Wherever we have erred or omitted something others may deem important, we ask indulgence.

I am indebted to all the members of the team who have shared their favorite hymn stories along with their personal experiences and observations. Lee Fisher, a gifted musician and Bible scholar, who has been an intimate friend and associate of Dr. Graham, gave invaluable help in checking the manuscripts.

A special word of thanks goes to my beloved colleague, Don Hustad, whose fellowship and musicianship has been a great source of inspiration to me. His unique gifts and abilities have well qualified him for the task of research and writing which he has untiringly pursued.

If the song of the Lord resounds more assuredly from your heart and life as a result of this little volume, all of the time and effort put into it will be worthwhile.

Yours, in the glad song our Saviour brings,

Cliff Barrows

May 4, 1967

I with thee would begin

[*Crusader Hymns*, No. 279]

A Hymn Story by Cliff Barrows

What a wonderful thing it is to be able to "begin again!" What if, having made a bad start in a subject in school or with a project at work, we were doomed to receive a failing grade or to be dismissed from our job? How much more tragic life would be if we could never recover from the bad starts we all make in moral and spiritual ways. In his poem "Birches" Robert Frost says: "I'd like to get away from earth awhile and then come back to it and begin over." The first part of his wish will never be realized; but we can all stay right where we are and begin over again.

This is one of the benefits that salvation brings. We can forget our old sins and failures because God has forgotten them. Through the prophet Jeremiah, God has said, "I will forgive their iniquity and I will remember their sin no more" (Jer. 31:34). The Bible talks about "books" (Dan. 7:10; Rev. 20:12) and suggests that all our shortcomings are recorded from the day of our birth. But when we accept Christ's offer of forgiveness, our embarrassing and condemning record is blotted out. In a past generation they would have said, "The slate was wiped clean."

More than this, we are given a completely new nature — the nature of God — so that we need not be dominated by our weaknesses as we were before. In *Living Letters*, II Corinthians 5:17 reads this way: "When someone becomes a Christian he becomes a brand new person inside. He is not the same any more. A new life has begun."

Of course, we continue to make occasional "bad starts" throughout life. Even after Christ dwells within us, we may be tempted to err and spoil our record. But Christians too can "begin again." I John 1:7, 9 (*LL*) says: "If we are living in the light of God's presence, just as Christ does, then we have wonderful fellowship and joy with each other, and the blood of Jesus His Son cleanses us from every sin . . . If we confess our sins to Him, he can be depended on to forgive us our sins and to cleanse us from every wrong." Remember that John is writing here to Christians, to those who "are living in the light of God's presence."

Sometimes we hear the idea mentioned that, after a certain age, a person cannot change. It is true that our patterns of behavior are pretty well established when we are young. But it is also true that a man can change and be changed at any age, with the help of God. At any time in life, we can win victory over an attitude or a habit, and we can begin again.The Apostle Paul was probably thinking of some old failures of his own when he said, near the end of his life; "Forgetting the past and looking forward to what lies ahead, I strain to reach the end of the race" (Phil. 3:13, 14, *LL*).

Some folk talk about "turning over a new leaf" at the beginning of a new year. Others seem to be cynical about New Year's resolutions because they are often forgotten by the 5th of January. When this happens, it is either because we did not really mean to keep them or because we tried to do so in our own human strength. Only God can give us the power to change and to be changed.

Each morning is a good time to begin again. In our period of personal worship, we can ask God for strength and grace to live that day in victory, accomplishing all that we would like to do. And, if we find that we have failed by noon, even then we can begin again.

In its original form, this is a Swedish hymn whose author is unknown. Because the translation is literal, you may find that the sentence structure is occasionally inverted and the meaning is a bit obscure. But if you make the effort to understand, you will find that it is a prayer that we may start anew — right now — in the strength of Christ and with guidance from His Word. And if you take the trouble to sing it, you will enjoy its "Swedish style" melody.

[Read or sing the entire hymn.]

I with Thee would begin, O my Saviour so dear,
On the way that I still must pursue;
I with Thee would begin every day granted here,
As my earnest resolve I renew
To be and remain Thine forever.

I with Thee would begin and go forth in Thy name,
Which alone doth salvation bestow;
Fold me close to Thy breast where found joy all who came,
There is refuge for me too, I know,
Though all in this world is confusion.

Let Thy Word all-divine be my lamp, in whose light
I may constantly keep to Thy way;
And each day wouldst Thou cleanse me anew, make me white
In the blood shed for me on that day
The cross Thou didst suffer, Lord Jesus.

I with Thee would begin – yea, and hear one more prayer,
I would close with Thee too my brief day,
And when daylight has failed, let me sleep in Thy care,
Until waking Thy child Thou dost say,
"Come, live with me ever in heaven."

From the Swedish, anon.
Tr. by A. Samuel Wallgren (1885-1940)

Amazing grace! how sweet the sound,
That saved a wretch like me!
I once was lost, but now am found,
Was blind, but now I see.

'Twas grace that taught my heart to fear,
And grace my fears relieved;
How precious did that grace appear
The hour I first believed!

Through many dangers, toils and snares,
I have already come;
'Tis grace hath brought me safe thus far,
And grace will lead me home.

When we've been there ten thousand years,
Bright shining as the sun,
We've no less days to sing God's praise
Than when we first begun.

John Newton, 1-3 (1725-1807)
John P. Rees, 4 (ascribed) (1828-1900)

Amazing Grace! How Sweet the Sound

[*Crusader Hymns*, No. 108]

A Hymn Story by Billy Graham

One Sunday in 1966 during the Earls Court crusade in London, we were driving between speaking engagements in the university towns of Oxford and Cambridge. Suddenly I noticed that we were passing through the village of Olney and I remarked to my wife, "There's a famous church and graveyard here. Let's stop to visit them."

Riding through the Olney village square, we passed the former home of William Cowper. It is now a museum that houses the personal effects of that great English poet, to whom we are indebted for classic poetry as well as for some of our finest hymns. This village is also famous as the place where the Shrove Tuesday pancake races originated.

The Olney parish church of Saints Peter and Paul was built in the fourteenth century, but much of the original beauty and dignity remains. In the corner of the churchyard, almost overgrown with tall grass, we found what we were looking for — a large tombstone with these words inscribed:

> **John Newton, Clerk; once an infidel and libertine, a servant of slaves in Africa, was by the rich mercy of our Lord and Saviour Jesus Christ preserved, restored, pardoned, and appointed to preach the faith he had long labored to destroy.**

Newton was the son of a sea captain who was engaged in the Mediterranean trade. His mother died when he was six, and after only two years of formal schooling he joined his father's ship at the age of eleven. His early life was one of immorality, debauchery and failure. He was rejected by his father, in trouble with all his employers, and finally jailed and degraded. In later years he served on slave ships, where he so incurred the hatred of his employer's negro wife that he became virtually a "slave of slaves."

This miserable seaman was brought to his senses by reading Thomas a Kempis's book, *Imitation of Christ.* His actual conversion was the result of a violent storm in which he almost lost his life. At the age of thirty-nine, John Newton became a minister and gave the rest of his life to serving God in the church. During the fifteen years he was the pastor at Olney, he wrote many hymns. Together with William Cowper, he published a hymnal which was widely used in Anglican churches.

It seems to me that "Amazing Grace" is really Newton's own testimony of his conversion and of his life as a Christian. He might have begun the hymn with the first stanza of another of his poems, "He Died for Me," but these words have somehow dropped out of use:

In evil long I took delight,
Unawed by shame or fear,
Till a new object struck my sight,
And stopped my wild career.

"God's grace" has been defined as "His undeserved favor." It was this grace that reached out to John Newton. When he learned that Christ loved him and had died for him, he was amazed. It was this grace which made him conscious that he was a sinner ("grace taught my heart to fear") and then assured him that his sins were forgiven ("grace my fears relieved"). So it is with all of us. We are all "great sinners" not only because of transgressions committed, but also because we fall short of God's standard for our lives. And this "amazing grace" is available to all of us.
[Read or sing stanzas 1 and 2.]

As Christian believers we continue to experience God's undeserved love and favor throughout all of life. Every day He forgives our shortcomings, if we confess them. Every day He supplies all our needs.

John Newton never ceased to marvel at God's mercy and grace that had been granted to him. Over the mantelpiece in the Olney vicarage he had placed an inscription which still remains:

Since thou wast precious in my sight, thou hast been honourable (Isa. 43:4). But thou shalt remember that thou wast a bondman in the land of Egypt, and the Lord thy God redeemed thee (Deut. 15:15).

He never forgot the sea. Late in life, when he was pastor of St. Mary, Woolnoth in London, Newton entered the pulpit in the uniform of a sailor, with a Bible in one hand and a hymnbook in the other. His mind was failing then, and he sometimes had to be reminded what he was preaching about. When someone suggested that he should retire, he replied, "What, shall the old African blasphemer stop while he can speak?" On another occasion, he said, "My memory is nearly gone, but I remember two things: that I am a great sinner, and that Christ is a great Saviour."

They tell us that the last stanza of this song was not written by John Newton. But I think he would agree that it is a fitting climax to his testimony. After he – and we – have been in heaven for ten thousand years worshipping our Lord, we will still have endless time to sing of His amazing grace!
[Read or sing stanzas 3 and 4.]

How Great Thou Art

[*Crusader Hymns*, No. 1]

A Hymn Story by George Beverly Shea

During the London crusade at Harringay Arena in 1954, my friend, Mr. Andrew Gray, of the publishing firm Pickering and Inglis, Ltd., handed me a little four-page leaflet containing a "new hymn." We receive many contributions of this kind and at first I did not examine it closely. But I did notice that it had words in both English and Russian, and that it had a very strong and worshipful title, "How Great Thou Art."

A few weeks later I learned that this "new hymn" by S. K. Hine was the final result of almost seventy years of literary activity, involving several different writers and translators. It had first been written in Sweden in 1885 or 1886 by Rev. Carl Boberg, a well-known preacher and religious editor, who also served for fifteen years as a senator in the Swedish parliament. The original title was "O Store Gud" (O Great God).

An earlier translation into English was published in 1925 under the title "O Mighty God," but it never really caught on. "How Great Thou Art" arrived in America by a much more devious route! Retracing its history will allow the reader to share an interesting bit of hymn research.

The German version "Wie gross bist Du" had been translated from the original Swedish by Manfred von Glehn, a resident of Estonia, in 1907. Five years later, in 1912, the Rev. Ivan S. Prokhanoff—known as the "Martin Luther of modern Russia"—published the hymn in St. Petersburg in his own language, probably translating it from von Glehn's German poem. It is included in a booklet entitled "*Cymbals*"—"a collection of spiritual songs translated from various languages." The interesting title was derived from Psalm 150:5, "Praise him upon the loud cymbals: praise him upon the high sounding cymbals."

In 1922, several of Prokhanoff's hymn-booklets, including *Cymbals*, were combined in a large volume, *The Songs of a Christian*. It was published (in Russian) in New York City, by Prokhanoff's friends of the American Bible Society. Finally, in 1927, this larger book was reprinted in Russia, again through the assistance of Prokhanoff's American supporters. This new release of Russian evangelical hymns brought "How Great Thou Art" to the attention of an English missionary couple, Mr. and Mrs. Stuart K. Hine, and it was widely used by them in evangelism in the western Ukraine. After singing it for many years in Russian, Mr. Hine translated three verses into English. When the Second World War broke out, the Hines returned to Britain, where the fourth stanza was added in 1948.

The completed song was printed in 1949 in a Russian gospel magazine published by Mr. Hine. Reprints were requested by missionaries all over the world, and it was one of those leaflets that was given to us in 1954. We first sang "How Great Thou Art" in the Toronto, Canada Crusade of 1955. Cliff Barrows and his large volunteer choir assisted in the majestic refrains. Soon after, we used it on the "Hour of Decision" and in American crusades. In the New York meetings of 1957 the choir joined me in singing it ninety-nine times! It became a keynote of praise each evening.

Reading the first verses of this song of worship, we think of the opening words of Psalm 19: "The heavens declare the glory of God and the firmament showeth his handiwork." Carl Boberg once said that the inspiration for his original hymn was the beauty of the Swedish meadows and lakes, after a summer thunderstorm.

Stuart Hine has also written* that the first verse of his English version came to life after a memorable thunderstorm in a Carpathian mountain village in Czechoslovakia, where he had to seek shelter for the night. On a later occasion, he visited the mountain country of Bukovina in Romania, and in the grandeur of the "woods and forest glades" heard a group of young Christians burst instinctively into song, accompanied by their mandolins and guitars. The hymn they sang was "How Great Thou Art" with Prokhanoff's Russian text, and it was this experience which moved Hine to pen his second stanza.

[Read or sing stanzas 1 and 2.]

Yes, God talks to us through His creation — the heavens and the earth declare His glory. But the greatness of God is shown even more completely in the salvation He has planned and provided for us. What wisdom it reveals! What love it discloses! As the third stanza confesses, this greatness is more than I can understand; "I scarce can take it in."

Mr. Hine also says* that his final verse was written just after the Second World War, when many refugees from eastern Europe were streaming into England. Although they had found greater safety and freedom in their adopted land, their incessant question

*By permission. The author's complete and fascinating story of his writing of this hymn: *The Story of How Great Thou Art,* by Stuart K. Hine, "Carpathia", Coast Road, Berrow, Burnham-on-Sea, Somerset (England). Price: $.80

was "When are we going home?" It is only when we reach our heavenly home that we will fully comprehend the greatness of our God. As the Apostle Paul reminds us: "Now we see only puzzling reflections in a mirror, but then we shall see face to face. My knowledge now is partial; then it will be whole, like God's knowledge of me." (I Cor. 13:12, *New English Bible*). In that day we shall "bow in humble adoration" and say, "My God, how great Thou art!"
[Read or sing stanzas 3 and 4.]

O Lord my God, when I in awesome wonder
Consider all the worlds Thy hands have made,
I see the stars, I hear the rolling thunder,
Thy pow'r thro'out the universe displayed.

When through the woods and forest glades I wander
And hear the birds sing sweetly in the trees,
When I look down from lofty mountain grandeur,
And hear the brook and feel the gentle breeze.

And when I think that God, His Son not sparing,
Sent Him to die, I scarce can take it in,
That on the cross, my burden gladly bearing,
He bled and died to take away my sin.

When Christ shall come with shout of acclamation
And take me home, what joy shall fill my heart!
Then I shall bow in humble adoration,
And there proclaim, my God, how great Thou art.

Refrain:

Then sings my soul, my Saviour God, to Thee;
How great Thou art, how great Thou art!
Then sings my soul, my Saviour God, to Thee:
How great Thou art, how great Thou art!

Stuart K. Hine (b. 1899)

(This important song copyright has been handled in the United States by Mr. Tim Spencer, our longtime friend who was for many years president of the Hollywood Christian Group. Mr. Spencer has provided thousands of free copies of "How Great Thou Art" for use by Crusade Choirs and as souvenir editions for our radio and television audiences. *Editor.*)

All creatures of our God and King,
Lift up your voice and with us sing,
Alleluia! Alleluia!
Thou burning sun with golden beam,
Thou silver moon with softer gleam!
O praise Him, O praise Him,
Alleluia! Alleluia! Alleluia!

Thou rushing wind that art so strong,
Ye clouds that sail in heav'n along,
O praise Him! Alleluia!
Thou rising morn, in praise rejoice,
Ye lights of evening, find a voice!
O praise Him, O praise Him,
Alleluia! Alleluia! Alleluia!

Dear mother earth, who day by day
Unfoldest blessings on our way,
O praise Him! Alleluia!
The flow'rs and fruits that in thee grow,
Let them His glory also show!
O praise Him, O praise Him,
Alleluia! Alleluia! Alleluia!

And all ye men of tender heart,
Forgiving others, take your part,
O sing ye! Alleluia!
Ye who long pain and sorrow bear,
Praise God and on Him cast your care!
O praise Him, O praise Him,
Alleluia! Alleluia! Alleluia!

Let all things their Creator bless,
And worship Him in humbleness.
O praise Him! Alleluia!
Praise, praise the Father, praise the Son,
And praise the Spirit, Three in One!
O praise Him, O praise Him,
Alleluia! Alleluia! Alleluia!

St. Francis of Assisi (1182-1226)
Tr. by William H. Draper (1885-1933)

All Creatures of Our God and King

[*Crusader Hymns*, No. 16]

A Hymn Story by Tedd Smith

One of my favorite hymn tunes, and one that I often play in sacred concerts, is associated with what has been called "Nature's Hymn of Praise" — namely, "All Creatures of Our God and King." It was written by Francis of Assisi, one of the most interesting figures in all church history. The melody is of unknown origin, but was first published in a Roman Catholic hymnal in 1623.

Francis was born into the carefree life of a wealthy Italian family in 1182. At an early age he was converted to Jesus Christ. Renouncing his life of ease, he became an itinerant evangelist who roamed through the countryside, working with the peasants and preaching to them. He gathered about him a large group of followers with whom he toured the Mediterranean lands for fourteen years. The message he proclaimed was that love for Christ leads to a life of sacrifice and of brotherly love among men.

This "patron saint of animals" came to love God's world of nature, probably because he lived a simple life so close to it. His hymn expresses the truth that all creation praises its Creator. It may have been based on Psalm 145:10, 11: "All thy works shall praise thee, O Lord . . . They shall speak of the glory of thy kingdom, and talk of thy power."
[Read or sing stanza 1.]

The hymn is similar in form to the *Benedicite*, a traditional church canticle which is taken from the *Septuagint* version of the Scriptures. The *Benedicite* calls upon "showers and dew," "frost and cold," "lightnings and clouds," as well as "green things" and "fowls of the air" — to "bless the Lord." It begins with the words: "O all ye works of the Lord, bless ye the Lord; praise him and magnify him forever."

All earth's creatures derive life from God and depend on Him for the continuance of their existence. Inferior animals are not capable of knowing the Almighty, yet the Bible says that they "wait upon God" because they seek their food according to natural instinct. "That thou mayest give them their meat in due season...thou openest thine hand, they are filled with good" explains Psalm 104:27, 28. It is said that Saint Francis wrote these words during the hot summer of 1225 when he was very ill and losing his sight. To add to his discomfort, a swarm of field mice were trying to take over his little straw hut. No doubt he encouraged even the mice to praise God!

O all ye beasts and cattle: bless ye the Lord! (Benedicite)

It is not difficult to see that the cosmic universe shows the power and glory of God. As Psalm 97:6 says, "The heavens declare his righteousness, and all the people see his glory."

In our day, the telescope reveals much about space that was not known before. We are told that if our sun were hollow, it could hold more than a million worlds the size of our earth. But some of the remote stars are so vast that they could hold half a billion of our suns! There are about 100 billion stars in the average galaxy, and at least 100 million galaxies in *known* space. And many scientists believe that we have probed only one billionth of "theoretical space!"

O ye Sun and Moon, bless ye the Lord.

O ye stars of heaven, bless ye the Lord.

The microscope reveals that ours is a God of *little* things, as well. The ocean is teeming with tiny living forms called plankton. One variety of plankton is the *diatom*, a form of life related to seaweed. The diatom is so small that it would take 15 million to fill a thimble, yet each one is a marvel of beautiful and intricate design. Like the snowflakes, it seems that no two are alike!

O ye Whales and all that move in the waters: bless ye the Lord.

[Read or sing stanzas 2 and 3.]

And what of man, the crowning achievement of the creative acts of God? Is not human personality the outstanding marvel in a world of wonders? God has lavished more love and care on man than on all the rest of His world. Jesus said, "Are not two sparrows sold for a farthing? and one of them shall not fall on the ground without your Father... Fear ye not therefore, ye are of more value than many sparrows" (Matt. 10:29, 31).

Unlike the rest of God's creation, man has been given a soul and spirit with which he may know his Creator. He praises God in a way that is denied the rest of the universe—by responding to the love of God with his entire being!

O ye children of men: bless ye the Lord.

O ye holy and humble men of heart: bless ye the Lord. Praise Him and magnify Him forever!

[Read or sing stanzas 4 and 5.]

Guide Me, O Thou Great Jehovah

[*Crusader Hymns*, No. 213]

A Hymn Story by Don Hustad

The Welsh people may well be the most enthusiastic singers in the world. Their centuries-old tradition, that everybody loves to sing, has been perpetuated in the International Eisteddfodd which is held at Llangollen each year.

The Welsh miners customarily sang on their way to work in the coal pits. In the great spiritual revivals which have come to Wales several times during the past two hundred years, music was often more important than preaching. Their pastors and evangelists were never disturbed if the sermon was interrupted by a spontaneous outburst of congregational song. For it was often through singing that the Spirit of God moved the congregation to repentance and faith in Christ.

One of Wales' greatest hymn writers in the late eighteenth century was the layman-preacher William Williams. During forty years of ministry he traveled almost 100,000 miles, on foot and on horseback, preaching and singing. The best known of his 800 hymns is "Guide Me, O Thou Great Jehovah."

During a choir concert I conducted in Cardiff in 1954, we invited the congregation to join us in singing this hymn. After we had finished the stanzas we knew in English, someone in the audience led out in the Welsh version. On and on they sang, hymn after hymn, until we were almost unable to finish the choral program. Today, as in much of the world, the folk in Wales do not attend church as faithfully as they once did. But you will still hear them sing this hymn—just as we sing our national anthem—at the beginning of outdoor athletic events!

[Read or sing stanza 1.]

From the words of the first line, we understand that this is a prayer for God's care and guidance throughout life. It recalls incidents from the forty-year journey of Israel through the desert, after they had left Egypt for their trek to the promised land of Canaan. Although they were delayed in reaching their new home because of sin and unbelief, God continued to lead them and to provide for their needs each day of those forty years.

We too are pilgrims in a journey from the cradle to the grave, and many times our lives will seem like a "barren land," a wilderness. Many times in our weakness we call upon the mighty God to sustain us with His powerful hand. As He fed the children of Israel each day with manna — a supernatural "bread from heaven" — so He has promised to "supply our every need" (Phil. 4:19). We are nourished by the Word of God, which another hymn calls the "bread of life;" and it is God's written Word which tells of the "Word made flesh," Jesus Christ.

[Read or sing stanza 2.]

Twice, during the Hebrews' years of wandering, they became faint because they had no water. At the command of God, Moses struck a large rock with his wooden staff and out of it flowed a pure, crystalline stream which saved their lives. The apostle Paul once told the story and drew the same spiritual lesson as the hymn presents:

> **And by a miracle God sent them food to eat and water to drink there in the desert; they drank the water that Christ gave them. He was there with them as a mighty Rock of spiritual refreshment (I Cor. 10:3,4, *Living Letters*).**

God supplied the basic physical needs of the Hebrews. He also led them miraculously, day by day and step by step. During the day they followed a cloud which moved before the marching column; at night, the cloud appeared to be a "pillar of fire" which hung over the camp to remind them that God was there, watching over them. Even so, the Christian believer today may experience God's guidance in all the little things, as well as in the major decisions of life.

[Read or sing stanza 3.]

When the ancient Jewish pilgrims finally reached the Jordan river which formed the boundary of the promised Canaan, there too God was with them. Joshua 3:14-17 tells us that, when the people moved forward in faith, the river parted so that they could walk over "dry-shod." At the end of our life's journey, death may appear to be a river we dread to cross. But when Christ is our Lord, He walks with us through the waters of death and leads us with great happiness to the other side — our Canaan, our eternal home.

One of the joys of the Christian life is the consciousness that God is with us each moment, guiding, protecting, and providing. This is why we love to sing, with our brothers in Wales:

Songs of praises, songs of praises
I will ever give to Thee.

Guide me, O Thou great Jehovah,
Pilgrim through this barren land;
I am weak, but Thou art mighty;
Hold me with Thy powerful hand;
Bread of heaven, Bread of heaven,
Feed me till I want no more.

Open now the crystal fountain,
Whence the healing stream doth flow;
Let the fire and cloudy pillar
Lead me all my journey through;
Strong Deliverer, strong Deliverer,
Be Thou still my strength and shield.

When I tread the verge of Jordan,
Bid my anxious fears subside;
Death of death, and hell's destruction,
Land me safe on Canaan's side;
Songs of praises, songs of praises
I will ever give to Thee.

From the Welsh
Tr. by Peter Williams (1722-1796)
and William Williams (1717-1791)

Stand up, stand up for Jesus,
    Ye soldiers of the cross;
Lift high His royal banner,
    It must not suffer loss:
From victory unto victory
    His army shall He lead,
Till every foe is vanquished,
    And Christ is Lord indeed.

Stand up, stand up for Jesus,
    The trumpet call obey;
Forth to the mighty conflict,
    In this His glorious day:
"Ye that are men, now serve Him"
    Against unnumbered foes;
Let courage rise with danger,
    And strength to strength oppose.

Stand up, stand up for Jesus,
    The strife will not be long;
This day the noise of battle,
    The next, the victor's song:
To him that overcometh,
    A crown of life shall be:
He with the King of glory
    Shall reign eternally.

Refrain:

Stand up for Jesus,
    Ye soldiers of the cross;
Lift high His royal banner,
    It must not suffer loss.

George Duffield (1818-1888)

Stand Up, Stand Up for Jesus

[*Crusader Hymns*, No. 225]

The hymn "Stand Up, Stand Up for Jesus" was written by a Presbyterian minister, Rev. George Duffield, Jr., in memory of the heroic life and the early, tragic death of an Episcopalian rector, Dudley Tyng.

The year was 1854. At the age of twenty-nine, Dudley Tyng had already become rector of the Church of the Epiphany in Philadelphia. Behind him was a rich heritage of churchmanship. His grandfather had been an Episcopal bishop. His father was the distinguished pastor of the famous St. George's parish in New York City; before this, the elder Mr. Tyng had himself served the Epiphany congregation in Philadelphia. Dudley succeeded his father in the pulpit, well-trained both by tradition and by education at the University of Pennsylvania and the Episcopal Seminary at Alexandria, Virginia.

But Dudley Tyng was not a typical "fashionable church pastor." He believed firmly the doctrine that all men are sinners who need to repent and be converted if they are to be accepted by God. He also was convinced that slavery was immoral and unchristian, and he said so from the pulpit of his plush sanctuary. By the end of the second year in this ministry, Tyng's bold and straight-forward denunciation of sin so disturbed his cultured, wealthy parishioners that some were demanding his removal.

Supported by younger members of the congregation, he resigned from Epiphany and formed the "Church of the Covenant," which gathered to worship in a little meeting hall. The family went to live in their country home outside Philadelphia.

In addition to his responsibilities at the new church, young Dudley began giving noon lectures at the Philadelphia Y.M.C.A. Interest grew and thousands were converted to Christ. On Tuesday, March 30th, 1858, there was held an especially noteworthy service. Over five thousand men were gathered in Jayne's Hall, and Tyng preached from Exodus 10:11, "Ye that are men...serve the Lord." It was an eloquent, passionate and moving challenge that those present would never forget. Because he spoke so strongly, he asked pardon for anything that had offended his hearers. But he added, "I must tell my Master's errand, and I would rather that this right arm (placing his left hand on his right arm near the shoulder) were amputated at the trunk, than that I should come short of my duty to you in delivering God's message." Over one thousand men confessed Christ that day!

His words were strangely prophetic. The next week, while home on the farm, he stopped studying for a few moments and went out to the shed where a horse-powered corn sheller was working. Reaching out to stroke the animal, his clothing was caught in the cogs of the machine, severely mangling his arm. A few days later it was necessary to amputate.

The following week it became obvious that Tyng would not recover from the severe shock to his body. According to a Philadelphia newspaper, the dying man, with the same heroic spirit which never forsook him through all his sufferings, received the solemn announcement with the utmost resignation, answering only, "Then it is well, it is very well; God's will be done."

In the next few moments he urged his doctor to become a Christian, and begged his wife to encourage their boys to be ministers. Taking his venerable father, Dr. Stephen H. Tyng, by the hand, he said, "Stand up for Jesus; father, stand up for Jesus; and tell my brethren of the ministry, wherever you meet them, to stand up for Jesus!" And so he died.

The following Sunday, in the Temple Presbyterian Church, Tyng's friend George Duffield, Jr. preached on Ephesians 6:14, "Stand therefore, having your loins girt about with truth." At the end of the sermon he read the stanzas of this hymn, which he had written after the funeral.

As the thrust of the song implies, we Christian soldiers must wage a defensive, as well as an offensive warfare. It is often necessary to "stand fast" against evil as we seek to honor God. This is especially true today in view of the prevalent "relativity" in morals and waning faith in the Word of God. A faithful Christian must take the banner of absolute truth and absolute holiness, because this is the standard of God Himself.

The second stanza of the hymn paraphrases the text of Dudley Tyng's eloquent sermon in that memorable YMCA noonday meeting, in these words: "Ye that are men, now serve Him." It takes *real men* to stand up for Jesus in the office and the factory! It takes courageous women to stand up for Christ in the neighborhood and in the social club! It takes brave boys and girls to stand up for Jesus in the classroom and on the sports field!

[Read or sing the entire hymn.]

Love Divine, All Loves Excelling

[*Crusader Hymns*, No. 170]

A Hymn Story by Cliff Barrows

All of us have experienced the "lift" that comes with singing a great hymn together. Uniting our hearts and voices in Christian song gives us a sense of release over our fears and weaknesses.

This has been my experience over and over again. One of the instances which is still vivid to me happened in 1961, during the Manchester, England crusade. Just as the meetings were about to start, Billy Graham became quite seriously ill. Leighton Ford was called to be his substitute for the first week of crusade services.

Billy had been scheduled to speak to the ministers of London just before the crusade opened. You can imagine my feelings when he sent word that I should represent him and speak at that meeting. The British pastors are themselves thorough scholars and often brilliant preachers. And they were expecting to hear Billy Graham, not me!

At the beginning of that meeting in Westminster's Central Hall, the ministers joined in singing this great hymn of Charles Wesley. Most of these British clergymen were also well acquainted with hymn texts and hymn tunes, and they sang gloriously. Accompanied by the grand piano and the great pipe organ and using the Welsh tune "Blaenwern," these familiar words lifted our hearts in praise and prayer to God. I felt God's strength evident through the singing; He blessed our meeting together, despite my fears and their disappointment.
[Read or sing stanza 1.]

This is perhaps one of our most familiar hymns, and yet I fear that most Americans have only a vague notion of what it says. Reading only the title or the first line, we assume that it is a hymn extolling the love of God. But its message is far more specific than that.

Who is the "Joy of heaven, to earth come down?" It is Jesus Christ who comes to make our hearts His humble dwelling. The third line of the first stanza makes it clear. Jesus is "pure, unbounded love"—the love of God made manifest—the love of God incarnate, in the flesh. The hymn, then, is really a prayer to Christ who is Love Divine.
[Read or sing stanza 2.]

But there are still other obscure phrases in the hymn. What is "that second rest" that we are asking to find? Here it helps to know something of the doctrinal emphasis of the Wesleys and of all the early Methodists. They believed that after conversion there is a second experience for the Christian – that when one totally consecrates himself to Christ, his heart is cleansed from all sin. The experience is called "entire sanctification." They believe that an individual who is sanctified – "made holy" – experiences a relief from the struggle with sin in his life, and finds a new "rest" or liberty in Christ. This is the "second rest" mentioned in the hymn and it is derived from Hebrews 4:9, "There remaineth therefore a rest to the people of God." This also helps us understand the "Alpha and Omega" phrase in the second stanza. The two experiences of conversion and sanctification are thought of as the "*beginning* of faith" and the "*end* of faith."

We must admit that there are differences among Christians with regard to this doctrine of sanctification. But there is common agreement that when we reach the end of ourselves and yield our bodies and minds completely to God, we do find spiritual power and freedom that we cannot otherwise know. Many Christians of varied church backgrounds have witnessed that for them this was a single crisis experience that came after they first knew Jesus Christ as Saviour. Others would say that their act of consecration was repeated daily, and that, for them, "becoming holy" was a matter of progress and growth.

. Of course, for all Christians, any experience should be only the beginning of Christian maturing, of "growing in grace." We must all be changed "from glory to glory"—knowing more about Christ and becoming more like Him, until we "take our place in heaven."

And, let us not be afraid of the expression "Christian holiness." Actually it means more than freedom from sin – this is a negative concept that only partly explains the phrase. "Holiness" is really "wholeness" – a balanced personality that possesses all virtues and strengths, in body, mind and spirit. Spiritual "wholeness" or maturity is something we should all desire and seek.

[Read or sing stanzas 3 and 4.]

Love Divine, all loves excelling,
Joy of heav'n, to earth come down:
Fix in us Thy humble dwelling,
All Thy faithful mercies crown:
Jesus, Thou art all compassion,
Pure, unbounded love Thou art:
Visit us with Thy salvation;
Enter every trembling heart.

Breathe, O breathe Thy loving Spirit
Into every troubled breast!
Let us all in Thee inherit,
Let us find that second rest.
Take away our bent to sinning,
Alpha and Omega be;
End of faith, as its beginning,
Set our hearts at liberty.

Come, almighty to deliver,
Let us all Thy life receive;
Suddenly return, and never,
Nevermore Thy temples leave:
Thee we would be always blessing,
Serve Thee as Thy hosts above,
Pray and praise Thee without ceasing,
Glory in Thy perfect love.

Finish then Thy new creation,
Pure and spotless let us be;
Let us see Thy great salvation
Perfectly restored in Thee:
Changed from glory into glory,
Till in heav'n we take our place,
Till we cast our crowns before Thee,
Lost in wonder, love and praise.

Charles Wesley (1707-1788)

My Lord has garments so wondrous fine,
And myrrh their texture fills;
Its fragrance reached to this heart of mine,
With joy my being thrills.

His life had also its sorrows sore,
For aloes had a part;
And when I think of the cross He bore,
My eyes with teardrops start.

His garments too were in cassia dipped,
With healing in a touch;
Each time my feet in some sin have slipped,
He took me from its clutch.

In garments glorious He will come,
To open wide the door;
And I shall enter my heavenly home,
To dwell forevermore.

Refrain:

Out of the ivory palaces,
Into a world of woe,
Only His great, eternal love
Made my Saviour go.

Henry Barraclough (b. 1891)

IVORY PALACES

[*Crusader Hymns*, No. 86]

A Hymn Story by Billy Graham

The famous gospel song "Ivory Palaces" was written very near to my home in the mountains of North Carolina. In the summer of 1915 the famous evangelist Dr. J. Wilbur Chapman was preaching at the Presbyterian conference grounds at Montreat. With him were the songleader Charles M. Alexander, soloist Albert Brown, and their pianist Henry Barraclough. Barraclough, the author of this hymn, was a twenty-four-year-old Britisher; he had met Chapman the previous year during a preaching mission in England.

During the conference, the evangelist spoke one evening on the forty-fifth Psalm. He believed, as I do, that this is a prophetic, "Messianic" psalm which speaks of the relationship of Christ, the bridegroom, to His bride, the Church.

The eighth verse of the psalm was Dr. Chapman's text: "All thy garments smell of myrrh, and aloes, and cassia, out of the ivory palaces, whereby they have made thee glad." The oriental spices and perfumes mentioned here were used for many purposes. They were often poured on clothing so that their delightful odor seemed to be part of the very texture of the cloth. Following the suggestions of these provocative phrases, Dr. Chapman developed his sermon on the symbolism of the perfumed garments of an oriental bridegroom.

"Myrrh" was an exotic perfume associated with ecstasy and joy; it represents the beauty of the person of Christ — that beauty which attracts us to Him. "Aloes" was a bitter herb used in embalming, which should remind us that our Lord had many sorrows during His lifetime, culminating in a shameful and painful death on the cross. "Cassia" was a spicy perfume that was also a medication; Jesus Christ is like a potion that heals us from the wounds of sin when we look to Him in repentance.

After the evening service, "Charlie" Alexander and Henry Barraclough drove some friends to the Blue Ridge YMCA Hostel a few miles away. Sitting in the front seat of the car, young Barraclough thought about the message and the four short phrases of the refrain began to take shape in his mind. When they stopped at a little village store, he quickly wrote them down on a "visiting card" — the only paper that was available. Returning to the conference hotel, he worked out the first three stanzas, using the outline of Chapman's message. The following morning Mrs. Alexander and Mr. Brown sang the new hymn in the Montreat conference session.

Later, Dr. Chapman suggested that Barraclough add a fourth verse, reminding us that one day Christ will come again wearing the same glorious garments. I believe that through all eternity we will be reminded of the beauty of our Lord, of His suffering for us, and of the forgiveness and cleansing which He has made possible.

Henry Barraclough was not a prolific song writer. "Ivory Palaces" was his only masterpiece, but it has been sung around the world. After Dr. Chapman's death, Barraclough adopted the evangelist's country, America, as his own. He also became associated with Chapman's denomination and has served the Presbyterian Church (U.S.A.) for almost fifty years.

Our readers will be interested to learn that it was Albert Brown — one member of the duet that first sang "Ivory Palaces" — who first introduced Cliff Barrows to me in 1945. I was speaking at a youth night service at the Ben Lippen Conference Grounds in North Carolina. When the regular songleader could not appear, Mr. Brown suggested that we use two young musicians named Cliff and Billie Barrows who were visiting there on their honeymoon. That was the beginning of our many years of fellowship in God's service.

In our crusades today, "Bev" Shea often sings this hymn, sometimes accompanied by Cliff Barrows and the choir. We do not suppose that heaven actually consists of "ivory palaces;" this is merely the oriental imagery which is used to try to describe the beauty of our Lord's home, from which He departed to live among men on earth. Every time I hear this refrain, I am humbled by the truth that Jesus — the object of all the worship in heaven — willingly assumed all the limitations and suffering of a man. Why? Because He loved us so much.

Out of the ivory palaces,
Into a world of woe,
Only His great, eternal love
Made my Saviour go.

[Read or sing the entire hymn.]

holy, holy, holy

[*Crusader Hymns*, No. 8]

In the year that king Uzziah died I saw also the Lord sitting upon a throne, high and lifted up, and his train filled the temple. Above it stood the seraphims: each one had six wings; with twain he covered his face, and with twain he covered his feet, and with twain he did fly. And one cried unto another, and said, Holy, holy, holy, is the Lord of hosts: the whole earth is full of his glory. (Isaiah 6:1-3)

Although the Christian doctrine of the Trinity was not clearly understood before the day of Pentecost, we believe that it is revealed in the Old Testament as well as in the New. In this record of the prophet Isaiah's vision of God, the Trinity is suggested in the triple repetition of the angels, "Holy, holy, holy." These words have become one of the historic songs of believers in worship. It is called the *Trisagion* or the *Tersanctus*, the "three holies."

A parallel scripture passage is Revelation 4:8-11, of which this is the central phrase: "Holy, holy, holy, Lord God Almighty, which was, and is and is to come." The historic hymn "Holy, Holy, Holy" is based on these words. It was written by Reginald Heber to be sung on Trinity Sunday in the parish of Hodnet in western England. He was vicar there in his family's church from 1807 to 1823.

Heber was an uncommon man. Born into a family of wealth and culture, he gave his life to the service of God both at home in England and far away in India. Though he possessed unusual literary gifts and was a friend of Britain's leading men of letters, his greatest ambition was to improve the hymn singing in his own church.

When Reginald Heber accepted the post of Bishop of Calcutta in 1823, it was the realization of a longtime, deep-seated interest in foreign missions. As a bishop, Heber served a diocese that included much of the south Pacific. For three years he traveled tirelessly from place to place, using his remarkable gifts to advance the work of the church in that distant area. On April 3rd, 1826, Heber preached on the evils of the caste system before a large audience at Trichinopoly. Afterward, he went to cool off in the swimming pool at the home where he was staying. Some time later, he was found drowned, the result of a stroke.

At the age of forty-three his brilliant life was ended, and he was buried in the Anglican church at Trichinopoly. In 1875 the Prince of Wales (later Edward VII) honored his memory by placing a tablet there.

Reginald Heber lived and worked at a time in history when his contemporaries of English literature were becoming aware of the beauty of words and of poetic structure. The romantic movement of that day added a new dimension of elegance and lyric grace to Christian worship. This characteristic is never more evident than in Heber's hymn "Holy, Holy, Holy" which Lord Tennyson said was the greatest in the English language.

The powerful phrases of the hymn declare the attributes of the Triune God–Father, Son and Holy Spirit. Heber shows his mastery of poetic design in composing each stanza to re-emphasize the doctrine of the Trinity by using a "trinity of words" to say something about God. Stanza one mentions three of the attributes of God; He is "holy, merciful and mighty."

The second stanza reminds us that God is worshipped in heaven by the saints who have already died, and by the angels – "the cherubim and seraphim." It closes with a "trinity of phrases" which says that God is eternal – "He was, He is, and He evermore shall be."

God is also perfect. Our understanding of Him is incomplete; He is partially hidden by the "darkness" of our sin and our ignorance. Yet we can see enough of His glory to know that He is perfect – "perfect in power, in love, and purity." That is the "trinity" of the third stanza.

The final verse borrows another idea from John's vision as recorded in Revelation 4:11 – that God has created all things in the universe for "his own pleasure." Therefore, all creation – "the earth, the sky, and sea" – praises Him. This is Heber's final poetic trinity.

The tune commonly associated with these words was written by John B. Dykes, one of Britain's leading organists and composers, who was also an Anglican rector. When published in 1861, Dykes gave it the significant name "Nicaea." It was at the council of Nicaea in 325 A.D. that the church clearly enunciated its belief in the Trinity.

[Read or sing the entire hymn.]

Holy, Holy, Holy! Lord God Almighty!
    Early in the morning our song shall rise to Thee;
Holy, Holy, Holy! Merciful and Mighty!
    God in Three Persons, blessed Trinity!

Holy, Holy, Holy! All the saints adore Thee,
    Casting down their golden crowns around the glassy sea;
Cherubim and seraphim falling down before Thee,
    Which wert and art, and evermore shalt be.

Holy, Holy, Holy! Tho' the darkness hide Thee,
    Tho' the eye of sinful man Thy glory may not see,
Only Thou art holy; there is none beside Thee
    Perfect in power, in love, and purity.

Holy, Holy, Holy! Lord God Almighty!
    All Thy works shall praise Thy name, in earth, and sky, and sea;
Holy, Holy, Holy! Merciful and Mighty!
    God in Three Persons, blessed Trinity!

Reginald Heber (1783-1826)

"Great is Thy faithfulness," O God my Father,
There is no shadow of turning with Thee;
Thou changest not; Thy compassions, they fail not;
As Thou hast been Thou forever wilt be.

Summer and winter, and springtime and harvest,
Sun, moon and stars in their courses above,
Join with all nature in manifold witness
To Thy great faithfulness, mercy and love.

Pardon for sin and a peace that endureth,
Thy own dear presence to cheer and to guide;
Strength for today and bright hope for tomorrow,
Blessings all mine, with ten thousand beside!

Refrain:

"Great is Thy faithfulness! Great is Thy faithfulness!"
Morning by morning new mercies I see;
All I have needed Thy hand hath provided —
"Great is Thy faithfulness," Lord, unto me!

Thomas O. Chisholm (1866-1960)

Great Is Thy Faithfulness

[*Crusader Hymns*, No. 33]

A Hymn Story by George Beverly Shea

One of God's men who most influenced my life was Dr. Will H. Houghton, the late president of Moody Bible Institute. In 1938 when I was working in an insurance office in New York City and seeking to know what God wanted me to do with my life, Dr. Houghton asked me if I would like to come to Chicago and sing on the Institute's radio station, WMBI. One of our programs was "Hymns From the Chapel"—fifteen minutes of hymns at the early hour of 8:15 every morning. Along about 1942, Don Hustad joined me on the program, playing the organ.

I learned afterward that the program was often heard in those days by a young man named Billy Graham who was attending Wheaton College, just west of Chicago. A short time later, Billy asked me to help him in a broadcast from the Village Church in Western Springs where he was student pastor; this association led to our work together in the evangelistic crusades. How I thank God for His faithfulness in leading me one step at a time into His plan for my life!

Looking back, I remember also Dr. Houghton's tall, dark, commanding presence as he led Moody's chapel services with a wonderful combination of dignity, humor and song. He loved hymns and especially appreciated the song "Great Is Thy Faithfulness." Its music had been composed by William M. Runyan, who often appeared in person at the Institute in those days. Mr. Runyan later said that it was Dr. Houghton's frequent use of the hymn which helped it to become popular with the general public.

It would be wrong to assume that every hymn has been written or has become well known as the result of some dramatic experience. Some authors have simply made it a habit to write poems regularly, perhaps one every day. Out of the hundreds that flow from the pen, only a few will be worthy of publishing.

Thomas Chisholm, a Methodist life insurance agent, gave us these inspiring words. He says that there were no special circumstances surrounding their writing. He simply penned the lines from his impressions about God's faithfulness as told in the Bible and sent them, with several other poems, to his friend and collaborator William Runyan.

Our team had the privilege of introducing "Great Is Thy Faithfulness" to audiences in Great Britain in 1954; now the song is a favorite there too. It is often sung at British wedding services and was recently included in the new *Anglican Hymn Book* of 1965.

The opening stanza and refrain are taken directly from scriptural affirmations about God. "His compassions fail not. They are new every morning: great is thy faithfulness" (Lam. 3:22,23). "Every good gift and every perfect gift is from above, and cometh down from the Father of lights, with whom is no variableness, neither shadow of turning" (James 1:17). In other words, God is always like the bright sunlight characteristic of midday; there is never a shadow to cloud His complete and perfect faithfulness.

God's faithfulness derives from another attribute of His character—His immutability. This is our answer to a few so-called theologians in our day who proclaim that "God is dead." He *is* alive! He *is* eternal! He cannot change by so much as a shadow!
[Read or sing stanza 1 and refrain.]

In many ways nature shows us that God is faithful. Every sunset is followed by a sunrise. Every winter is followed by a summer. Whenever we plant seed, we can count on a harvest. In the sky we see innumerable stars all moving in patterns which can be charted by astronomers thousands of years in advance.

But even more clearly, through His dealings with mortal men, we have learned that God is faithful. He has promised in His Word to forgive our sins and to give us peace of mind and heart; when we accept Christ His Son as our Lord and Saviour, He fulfills His pledge. Morning by morning, day after day, we feel His presence in our hearts. Surely we can look forward with hope to His presence, even at the end of life's journey.

I am often reassured by these words of an unknown believer: "Fear not tomorrow, for God is already there!"
[Read or sing stanzas 2 and 3.]

Just As I Am, Without One Plea

[*Crusader Hymns*, No. 57]

A Hymn Story by Billy Graham

When I was converted in 1937 under the ministry of the evangelist Mordecai Hamm, two invitation songs were used and a total of eight stanzas were sung. I did not respond to the invitation until the final verse of the second song, and I have always been grateful that the evangelist waited so patiently. One of these hymns was "Just As I Am, Without One Plea."

We use this hymn today in almost every one of our crusades. Some critics object to singing at the time of the invitation because they claim it has an excessive emotional impact on the audience. But on the occasions when we use no music at all, others complain about the "impressive, dramatic silence" that is broken only by the footsteps of those who are coming forward.

There are several reasons why we choose the hymn "Just As I Am" for use at this most important moment in a crusade service. For one thing, it rings with a strong, positive note. Other songs give Christ's invitation just as clearly, but this one keeps repeating the affirmative response, "O Lamb of God, I come." The choir sings it while the people are walking down the long aisle or across the turf of an outdoor stadium, and the hymn verbalizes just what each of them is doing.

This song also presents the strongest possible Biblical basis for the call of Christ. It repeats many of the reasons a person should respond when the Spirit of God speaks to him. The first stanza, like most great hymns, has captured the truth of the entire hymn. We should feel free to come to God because He has invited us to come, and because Jesus died on the cross in order to reconcile us to His Father.

All men who come into the world—whether in Christian or pagan, civilized or primitive cultures—have the same innate awareness of God. They want to approach God and to be accepted by Him. The book of Genesis tells us that Cain, son of Adam, came to God with an offering of fruit and grain produced through his own hard work, but God did not recognize him. His brother Abel's approach to worship was with the sacrifice of an animal, as God had decreed; he was welcomed and accepted by God.

Today as well, men cannot apparently give up the idea that God will accept them because they "are good and decent" or because they have done good works for others or for the church. But the Bible says that we have "no plea" before God—no claim on His love or His forgiveness—except that Jesus Christ shed His blood for us. God accepts the sacrifice made by His own sinless Son.

In coming to Christ we should not wait until we have straightened out our lives a bit. No small improvement we can effect will make us any more acceptable to Him. God loves us just as we are and we should come that way.

We should also come to Christ because He alone can solve the problems of our lives. Only He can free us from our sense of guilt and from our mental frustrations and anguish. Only He can pardon and cleanse us, in order to make us presentable before God.

We should come to Christ even though we don't understand all about salvation. I believe that God has designed His offer so it is necessary to take a final leap of faith to bridge the gulf of things we cannot comprehend. It is interesting to learn that Charlotte Elliott, author of this hymn, was an invalid during much of her life and that these words were written to express her victory over spiritual doubt.

The year was 1834 and Miss Elliott was living in Brighton in her native England. She was forty-five years old and had been a devoted Christian for many years. Even so, she was plagued with unhappiness because of her seeming uselessness, for everyone around her was busy in the service of God. In her extreme depression she was tempted to doubt the reality of her spiritual life.

Gathering strength and resolve, Charlotte Elliott deliberately wrote down the reasons for her trust in Christ. This hymn was the result. In the ensuing years, countless Christians have shared her experience and renewed their faith over and over through these familiar words.

[Read or sing the entire hymn.]

When I come to present my credentials at the gate of heaven, it will mean nothing that I have traveled around the world preaching the gospel. Then, as when I was first converted, I will say:

Just as I am, without one plea,
But that Thy blood was shed for me,
And that Thou bidd'st me come to Thee,
O Lamb of God, I come.

Just as I am, without one plea,
    But that Thy blood was shed for me,
And that Thou bidd'st me come to Thee,
    O Lamb of God, I come! I come!

Just as I am, and waiting not
    To rid my soul of one dark blot,
To Thee whose blood can cleanse each spot,
    O Lamb of God, I come! I come!

Just as I am, though tossed about
    With many a conflict, many a doubt,
Fightings and fears within, without,
    O Lamb of God, I come! I come!

Just as I am, poor, wretched, blind;
    Sight, riches, healing of the mind,
Yea, all I need, in Thee I find,
    O Lamb of God, I come! I come!

Just as I am, Thou wilt receive,
    Wilt welcome, pardon, cleanse, relieve;
Because Thy promise I believe,
    O Lamb of God, I come! I come!

Charlotte Elliott (1789-1871)

Make me a captive, Lord,
And then I shall be free;
Force me to render up my sword,
And I shall conqueror be;
I sink in life's alarms
When by myself I stand;
Imprison me within Thine arms,
And strong shall be my hand.

My heart is weak and poor
Until it master find;
It has no spring of action sure –
It varies with the wind;
It cannot freely move
Till Thou hast wrought its chain;
Enslave it with Thy matchless love,
And deathless it shall reign.

My pow'r is faint and low
Till I have learned to serve:
It wants the needed fire to glow,
It wants the breeze to nerve;
It cannot drive the world
Until itself be driv'n;
Its flag can only be unfurled
When Thou shalt breathe from heav'n.

My will is not my own
Till Thou hast made it Thine;
If it would reach the monarch's throne
It must its crown resign:
It only stands unbent,
Amid the clashing strife,
When on Thy bosom it has leaned,
And found in Thee its life.

George Matheson (1842-1906)

Make Me a Captive, Lord

[*Crusader Hymns*, No. 141]

A Hymn Story by Don Hustad

[Read or sing stanza 1.]

It may be that the opening phrases of this hymn are quite puzzling to some readers. "Make me a captive, Lord, and then I shall be free; Force me to render up my sword, and I shall conqueror be." One may ask, "How is it possible to be slave and free, winner and loser, at the same time?"

This kind of a statement is called a "paradox"—a declaration that is true, yet seemingly self-contradictory or absurd. A few years ago I wrote new music for these words. Remembering the message of the hymn I called the tune "Paradoxy."

There are many paradoxes in the Bible. "When I am weak, then am I strong" (II Cor. 12:10). "Whosoever will save his life shall lose it" (Matt. 16:25). "He that is least among you all, the same shall be great" (Luke 9:48). Perhaps each of these verses expresses a different aspect of the same spiritual truth.

I think this paradoxical idea can be illustrated by the relationship of marriage. At the wedding altar, two persons give themselves to each other. They promise to "forsake all others" and "to love and to cherish." They have obligated themselves "till death do us part"—almost like slaves, and we jokingly say that they have lost their freedom. Yet the poet Shelley calls human love "that sweet bondage which is freedom's self."

When two individuals share each other's lives in this way, giving and receiving true love, each finds greater fulfillment and self-expression than he could ever have known alone. In subjugating his own will to the desires of the other, each discovers that his own character has been developed. In the bondage of marriage, they both find freedom!

This truth about our relationship to God is illustrated in a more striking way in John 12:24: "Verily, verily, I say unto you, Except a corn of wheat fall into the ground and die, it abideth alone: but if it die, it bringeth forth much fruit." Here is one of nature's phenomena; a kernel of wheat must disintegrate and decompose in the ground in order to reproduce itself. It must die in order that it might continue to live! Of course, Jesus was referring here to His own death and the many new lives which it would produce.

However, in the next verse (John 12:25) He applies this truth to each of us. "He that loveth his life shall lose it; and he that hateth his life in this world shall keep it unto life eternal." We too must "die" to our own ambitions and desires if we are to produce spiritual fruit in our lives. This is what George Matheson says over and over in his hymn. We are weak human beings, and we gain strength only when Christ becomes our Master. We will rule over our own minds and bodies and find greatest self-fulfillment, only when we become His slaves.

No doubt the hymn's writer George Matheson learned this lesson, at least partly, through his own personal experience. As a brilliant young ministerial student of eighteen, he lost his sight almost completely. Because of his blindness, he eventually had to give up his research and scholarship in the field of apologetic theology, an activity which he dearly loved and for which he had great talent.

Instead, George Matheson gave his time and strength to devotional preaching and writing. During his lifetime as a minister in the Scottish Free Church, he had a profound influence on all who heard him preach, including Queen Victoria. Through his writings, God's truth has transformed the lives of many, right down to the present day.

Though he was physically sightless, Matheson could read the hearts of men and women. He could also see God in a way that few are able to do—and seeing God, he became more God-like. No doubt he would want to add another paradox to our list: "When I became blind, I really began to see!"

[Read or sing stanzas 2-4.]

What a Friend We Have in Jesus

[*Crusader Hymns*, No. 185]

Henry Brooks Adams (1838-1918) once said: "One friend in a lifetime is much; two are many; three are hardly possible." Does that seem to be a bit of an exaggeration? After all, if we are at all socially compatible, most of us have several friends. Or do we? Real friends, that is.

Begin with the definition, "A friend is a person who knows all about us, yet loves us just the same." That idea probably disqualifies a few. Because if we were to openly exhibit our inward selves — the thoughts which reveal our insecurities and prejudices —we would probably lose contact with many of the people we consider to be our "friends."

What if our home should be broken by divorce? Or what if we should suddenly be overtaken by temptation and commit some serious sin? Would the people we now call "friends" stand by us through disgrace?

How many of our friendships are dependent upon social position or financial status? We entertain and are entertained by the folk who live at our social level, who attend our church and live in our community. What if our financial situation should change — either for better or for worse — causing us to move to a different social and economic level? Would our old friendships bridge the gap of that change? Possibly not.

These questions are not intended to cause us to view all our present friendships with suspicion. But they should remind us of the gracious words Jesus spoke to His disciples, "Henceforth I call you not servants; for the servant knoweth not what his lord doeth: but I have called you friends; for all things that I have heard of my Father I have made known unto you (John 15:15).

Some of us Christians are tempted to believe that if a friend falls into sin — whether it be moral downfall or theological doubt — he must be dropped, lest our reputations be sullied by his failure. But Jesus proved Himself to be a "friend of publicans and sinners" (Luke 7:34). His is a friendship which reaches down and lifts us up from sin and brings us into His own heavenly family. "What a friend we have in Jesus — all our sins and griefs to bear!"

[Read or sing stanza 1.]

For most of us, continuing friendship depends on a delicate balance of "give and take." If our "friend" should snub us, or ask too often for a favor, or fail to reciprocate adequately, the relationship would be jeopardized. But not so with Christ; it is not possible to "presume on His friendship." He stands ever ready to forgive us, no matter how often we may slight Him. He is a Friend who hears every request, and answers each time in just the way that is best for us.

[Read or sing stanza 2.]

Joseph Scriven, author of this hymn, was a man who experienced the friendship of Christ during a life filled with trouble. As a young man in Ireland, about 1840, his intended bride was accidentally drowned the evening before their wedding. He had begun training as a military cadet, but poor health forced him to abandon his dreams of a career in this field.

Moving to Canada, he became a servant of the underprivileged, helping those who were physically handicapped and financially destitute. But tragedy continued to stalk his steps. Once again, the plans for a wedding were cut short when his second fiancee died following a brief illness. It seemed that Joseph Scriven was destined to go through life alone, knowing only the friendship of Jesus Christ.

Through much of his life he experienced loneliness, meager pay for menial work, and physical illness. This hymn is his testimony that prayer does not necessarily eliminate trouble from our lives. But, in the midst of tragedy, temptations and weakness, Christ will be our ever-present Friend who will give us peace, "take and shield us," and carry our "load of care."

[Read or sing stanza 3.]

After his death, in recognition of his sacrificial service to others, a monument was erected at Port Hope, Ontario in tribute to Joseph Scriven, an Irish immigrant who was a friend to many and who found a friend in Jesus.

Here is an interesting footnote to our song's story. Charles Converse, the composer of this familiar melody, was no "mere gospel song writer." In early life he had studied serious art music in Germany where he counted the great composers Franz Liszt and Louis Spohr among his friends. Later he became a very successful lawyer. Even though he had written symphonies and oratorios, Converse enjoyed writing simple melodies for gospel songs. This is one that is known and loved around the world.

What a Friend we have in Jesus,
All our sins and griefs to bear!
What a privilege to carry
Everything to God in prayer!
O what peace we often forfeit,
O what needless pain we bear,
All because we do not carry
Everything to God in prayer!

Have we trials and temptations?
Is there trouble anywhere?
We should never be discouraged,
Take it to the Lord in prayer.
Can we find a friend so faithful
Who will all our sorrows share?
Jesus knows our every weakness,
Take it to the Lord in prayer.

Are we weak and heavy-laden,
Cumbered with a load of care?
Precious Saviour, still our refuge –
Take it to the Lord in prayer.
Do thy friends despise, forsake thee?
Take it to the Lord in prayer;
In His arms He'll take and shield thee,
Thou wilt find a solace there.

Joseph Scriven (1819-1886)

Refrain:
All glory, laud, and honor
To Thee, Redeemer, King,
To whom the lips of children
Make sweet hosannas ring.

Thou art the King of Israel,
Thou, David's royal Son,
Who in the Lord's name comest,
The King and Blessed One.

The company of angels
Are praising Thee on high,
And mortal men, and all things
Created, make reply.

The people of the Hebrews
With palms before Thee went;
Our praise and prayer and anthems
Before Thee we present.

To Thee, before Thy passion,
They sang their hymns of praise;
To Thee, now high exalted,
Our melody we raise.

Thou didst accept their praises;
Accept the prayers we bring,
Who in all good delightest,
Thou good and gracious King.

Theodulph of Orleans (760-821)
Tr. by John Mason Neale (1818-1866)

All Glory, Laud, and Honor

[*Crusader Hymns*, No. 270]

On Palm Sunday morning, an interesting bit of pageantry takes place in some liturgical churches. As the opening processional moves around the sanctuary, it will pause in one corner, and a soloist or a small group of the choir will sing the ancient Latin canticle *Gloria, laus et honor* or its English equivalent "All Glory, Laud and Honor." When the song is completed, the processional moves on and the service continues. This tradition may be based only upon a legend, but it has been perpetuated for more than a thousand years.

It is said that in the year 821 King Louis the Pious, son of Charlemagne, was participating in the Palm Sunday procession through the streets of Angers in the region of Orleans. As the parade stopped near a prison tower, suddenly a melodious voice was heard singing "Gloria, laus et honor." The emperor learned that the vocalist was Theodulph of Orleans, a great pastor, bishop and poet whom he had jailed on suspicion of treachery against the crown. Whereupon, so the story goes, "the gentle and merciful monarch was moved with compassion, and from that hour he delivered and pardoned him, and sent him back to his church, quit and absolved of the crime whereof he had been accused."

There are puzzling aspects to the story of Jesus' "triumphal" entry into Jerusalem, the event we remember on this Sunday of the church year. Four hundred fifty years earlier the prophet Zechariah had written: "Rejoice greatly, O daughter of Zion; shout, O daughter of Jerusalem: behold, thy King cometh unto thee: he is just, and having salvation; lowly, and riding upon an ass, and upon a colt the foal of an ass" (Zech. 9:9). Yet it is quite probable that those who waved the palms never knew that they were fulfilling prophecy.

Jesus was offering Himself to the Jews as their promised Messiah and King. But they desired and expected a mighty deliverer who would rescue them from the legions of Rome and restore to them the glory of their ancient kingdom. Many of them were attracted by the miracles which Jesus had performed, and therefore were willing to join the shouting crowds that day. But when they were asked about His identity they said only, "This is Jesus, the prophet of Nazareth, of Galilee." No Messiah, no king, no promised deliverer; just Jesus, a prophet of Nazareth.

Of course, our Lord's disciples — at least some of them — had recognized Him. Several weeks earlier, Simon Peter had said to Him, "Thou art the Christ, the Son of the living God" (Matt. 16:16). It may be that it was the disciples (see Luke 19:37-38) who started the chant that day, "Hosanna to the son of David: Blessed is he that cometh in the name of the Lord; Hosanna in the highest" (Matt. 21:9). Many of the multitude joined in the cry, possibly without fully realizing what they were saying. Doubtless, some of the same people were part of another crowd which, only a few days later, shouted: "Crucify him! Crucify him!"

There will be many in our churches today, repeating these verses of praise, whose singing will be as meaningless as it was many years ago. If we are to praise Christ properly, He must be King in our hearts and Lord of our lives — sovereign over body, mind and spirit. Because the ancient Hebrews were not prepared to accept Him as "spiritual King," Jesus knew that it was not time to be their temporal ruler. But the day will come when He will return as a glorious Monarch. Revelation 19:11,16 pictures Him as seated on a white horse; and "he . . . was called Faithful and True . . . And he hath on his vesture and on his thigh a name written, KING OF KINGS, AND LORD OF LORDS."

Christ desires our praise and our adoration; He deserves it, and He knows that it is through worship that our lives are purified and made complete. When the Pharisees asked Jesus to restrain His disciples in their jubilant praise, He said, "I tell you that, if these should hold their peace, the stones would immediately cry out." Yes, Jesus must be praised; nature will do it if man will not!

Today, let us join with the children of that first Palm Sunday, with all those who truly accepted Him as Lord, with the angels on high, and with the saints of all ages, singing "All glory, laud and honor to Thee, Redeemer, King."

[Read or sing the entire hymn.]

When I Survey the Wondrous Cross

[*Crusader Hymns,* No. 70]

A Hymn Story by Tedd Smith

One of the most important names in English hymnody is that of Isaac Watts. Born into a merchant's home in Southampton in 1674, Watts was sickly and rather unattractive as a child. At the same time by today's standards he was very precocious. Young Isaac began to study Latin at the age of four, and added Greek when he was nine, French at eleven and Hebrew at thirteen!

Watts was also interested in poetry, and it is said that much of his boyish talk came out in rhyme and meter. His father soon tired of conversation of this nature and outlawed the poetic improvising. But Isaac was irrepressible, and to enforce this prohibition, his father resorted to a spanking. Through his tears the boy cried:

"O father, do some pity take,
And I will no more verses make."

When he was fifteen, the young poet turned his talents to the service of the church. At that time, Christians in England sang nothing but strict and rather stilted versions of the Old Testament Psalms, introduced line after line by a "precentor" and repeated line after line by the congregation. Said Watts: "The singing of God's praise is the part of worship nighest heaven, and its performance among us is the worst on earth." Whereupon his father, a leading deacon in the Congregational church, charged him: "Young man, give us something better!"

Isaac Watts accepted the challenge and launched an avocation which earned him the title, "the father of English hymnody." As a Congregationalist minister he wrote over six hundred hymns, including the magnificent "When I Survey the Wondrous Cross."

Throughout the years this hymn has been acclaimed. It was ranked as "one of the four which stand at the head of all hymns in the English language" by John Julian, our greatest hymnologist. Many people would agree that it is the *very best* English hymn, a claim made by the nineteenth-century literary critic, Matthew Arnold.

In crusade services and in concerts, I often play two tunes which have been associated with these words. The tune "Hamburg" is best known in America and was written in 1824 by one of our own important musicians, Lowell Mason, when he was living in Savannah, Georgia. This simple yet solemn melody uses only five notes and is based on an ancient Gregorian "tone" or scale. I also enjoy playing the tune "Rockingham" which we sing more often in British crusades. This tune was published in 1790 by Edward Miller; its actual composer is not known. I believe that these two melodies bring out the different meanings of the words of the hymn's stanzas.

It seems to me that Isaac Watts wrote this text as if he were standing at the foot of Christ's cross, together with the disciple John, the faithful women, Jesus' mother, the Roman soldiers and the excited, shouting mob. When I play or sing the hymn, I try to make Watts' ideas and words my own. With him, I cannot help but marvel at the incredulity of the scene — the "Prince of heaven" nailed to a tree by sinful men. Jesus, dying for me! For it was my sins which He bore on that terrible day. Therefore, my voice was one of those which had cried, in Pilate's court, "Crucify him!" My hand — as well as the hand of the Roman soldier — had wielded the hammer which drove the nails into His body.

Then, in my mind's eye, I see the blood which flowed from His wounds, showing — as the hymn suggests — His sorrow because of my sins and also His great love for me. How can I fail to say, "God forbid that I should boast of anything but the cross of our Lord Jesus Christ, through which the world is crucified to me and I to the world" (Gal. 6:14, *New English Bible*).

It is difficult to understand the latter part of this scripture verse, but Watts explains it in the last stanza of his hymn. Our Lord does not want me to try to repay Him for His love and His sacrifice with my own sorrow, my good works, or with my material things. If I owned the "whole realm of nature," it wouldn't be enough to give Him in return. Christ wants *more* than this! He wants *me* — "my soul, my life, my all."

When you read this hymn, I hope that you will make the words and their meaning your very own, as I have done. If you sing it, I hope you will try both tunes. They are found on the same page in *Crusader Hymns*, numbers 70 and 71.

[Read or sing the entire hymn.]

When I survey the wondrous cross,
    On which the Prince of glory died,
My richest gain I count but loss,
    And pour contempt on all my pride.

Forbid it, Lord, that I should boast,
    Save in the death of Christ, my God;
All the vain things that charm me most
    I sacrifice them to His blood.

See, from His head, His hands, His feet,
    Sorrow and love flow mingled down;
Did e'er such love and sorrow meet,
    Or thorns compose so rich a crown?

Were the whole realm of nature mine,
    That were a present far too small;
Love so amazing, so divine,
    Demands my soul, my life, my all.

Isaac Watts (1674-1748)

I come to the garden alone,
    While the dew is still on the roses;
And the voice I hear, falling on my ear,
    The Son of God discloses.

He speaks, and the sound of His voice
    Is so sweet the birds hush their singing,
And the melody that He gave to me,
    Within my heart is ringing.

I'd stay in the garden with Him
    Though the night around me be falling,
But He bids me go; through the voice of woe,
    His voice to me is calling.

Refrain:

And He walks with me, and He talks with me,
    And He tells me I am His own,
And the joy we share as we tarry there,
    None other has ever known.

C. Austin Miles (1868-1946)

In the Garden

[*Crusader Hymns*, No. 196]

A Hymn Story by Don Hustad

Changing trends in church music was the discussion topic at a dinner party I attended a few years ago on a seminary campus. The wife of a theology professor complained that song leaders and choir directors seem to ignore many favorite hymns, such as "In The Garden."

"You don't sing the old favorites that we learned as youngsters," she said. "I've even heard some church musicians criticize 'In the Garden' as 'sentimental and meaningless'."

I couldn't resist the temptation. "What garden?" I asked.

"What difference does it make 'what garden'?" she retorted, with just a little heat.

The truth is—it makes quite a lot of difference. If the hymn is just a childhood favorite with pleasant phrases about gardens and birds and roses, it cannot be really meaningful in a vital worship experience today. This kind of an attachment for a song is a superficial emotion which is a good example of what we call "sentimentality."

But it doesn't have to be that way. There was a garden, and the hymn can be meaningful! C. Austin Miles, the composer, gives us the clue himself:

> **One day in March, 1912, I was seated in the darkroom where I kept my photographic equipment and organ. I drew my Bible toward me; it opened at my favorite chapter, John 20... That meeting of Jesus and Mary had lost none of its power to charm.**
>
> **As I read it that day, I seemed to be part of the scene. I became a silent witness to that dramatic moment in Mary's life, when she knelt before her Lord, and cried, 'Rabboni!'... Under the inspiration of this vision I wrote as quickly as the words could be formed the poem exactly as it has since appeared. That same evening I wrote the music. (From *Forty Gospel Hymn Stories*, by George W. Sanville).**

The specific reference to a garden becomes much clearer when we learn that C. Austin Miles was writing about the first Easter morning and the garden in which Jesus was buried. It was here Mary Magdalene came alone very early, "while the dew was still on the roses." When Jesus first spoke to her, she thought it was the gardener; but when He called her by name, she recognized His voice.

It is difficult to imagine what Mary's feelings and actions were at that moment. She had seen Jesus die on the cross. She was now coming to anoint His dead body with spices. But there He was, standing before her and talking to her. He was alive! She may have been startled at first, but when His identity became clear, she was filled with joy – as the song says, like a melody ringing in her heart! No doubt Mary wanted nothing more than to stay there in the garden with Jesus, but He ordered her to go and tell His disciples what had happened.

Mary's experience is relived by every person who confronts the risen Christ and realizes His presence in the routine of daily life. We too can "walk and talk" with Christ and be assured that we belong to Him. This experience is very real to a believer and brings a joy that is beyond any other satisfaction. Indeed, it may sometimes seem that no one else has ever known as much delight as we experience, walking each day with Christ. At least, this was author Miles' conviction when he wrote: "The joy we share as we tarry there, None other has ever known."

When we take time to know Christ intimately through prayer and meditation, we too may feel that we want to stay in His presence forever. But He "bids us go" as He did Mary, to tell others of His death, His resurrection and ascension, and His promise of coming again. His command to go is, in a sense, a "voice of woe" because men must be warned to turn from their sins if they are to escape God's judgment. And we are the only messengers God has to take this news to the world. As Paul the Apostle said: "Woe is unto me, if I preach not the gospel!" (I Cor. 9:16).

"In the Garden" was a favorite song during the days Homer Rodeheaver led singing for the Billy Sunday campaigns. It can be just as significant today if we remember its true meaning as we sing.

[Read or sing the entire hymn.]

Blessed Assurance

[*Crusader Hymns*, No. 97]

A Hymn Story by Cliff Barrows

Several years ago I stood in a cemetery at Bridgeport, Connecticut and looked at an unpretentious gravestone marked "Aunt Fanny." I recalled the life of a remarkable woman blind almost from birth who was probably the most important gospel song writer of the last hundred years. How many people have been won to faith in Christ by the hymns of Fanny Crosby!

One of Miss Crosby's close friends was Mrs. Joseph Knapp, wife of the founder of the Metropolitan Life Insurance Company of New York. Mrs. Knapp was an amateur musician, and on one of her visits to the blind poetess she brought a melody she had composed.

"What does the tune say?" she asked Fanny Crosby, after playing it a few times. The blind woman responded immediately:

Blessed assurance, Jesus is mine!
Oh, what a foretaste of glory divine!
Heir of salvation, purchase of God,
Born of His Spirit, washed in His blood.

This method of composing words to an existing tune became a habit, and Miss Crosby used it in writing many of her seven thousand songs.

During the ministry of the crusades and the "Hour of Decision" broadcasts, several hymns have been used as "theme songs." "Blessed Assurance" is one that seems to have lasted longer than the others. It has always been a favorite of mine. It is an ideal song of testimony which tells the unending peace and joy of the person who knows that God has accepted him because of what Jesus Christ has done on his behalf.

As well as I can remember, we began to use this song with crusade choirs as early as 1948 in such places as Ocean City, New Jersey and Baltimore, Maryland. My wife Billie was playing the organ then—our family had not yet arrived to keep her at home—and together we worked out the changes of tempo and the high ending which have become a trademark of crusade music.

[Read or sing stanzas 1 and 2.]

Admittedly, "Blessed Assurance" does not seem to have a clear outline or progression of thought. It is not a strong doctrinal presentation. Rather, it is a succession of completely personal, almost rambling expressions by an individual who *knows* that he has found new life in Christ. In his happiness and freedom he sings "Blessed assurance, Jesus is mine!" He is convinced that he has experienced a sample of heaven—a "foretaste of glory."

Both the second and third stanzas begin with the reminder that when we truly accept Jesus as Lord, we submit our wills to Him. At first this may seem to mean that we have lost our personal freedom. But we soon discover that this yielded life brings peace and rest, "delight and rapture."

Some folk criticize our simple gospel songs by claiming that they are too selfish and personal in content. But becoming a Christian is a completely personal thing. I was converted when, as a teenager, it dawned on me that John 3:16 could be read this way: "For God so loved Cliff, that He gave His only begotten Son, that if Cliff would believe on Him, he would have everlasting life."

This is why I love to sing, "This is *my* story, this is *my* song, Praising *my* Saviour all the day long."
[Read or sing stanza 3.]

There is one short quotation on the side of Fanny Crosby's gravestone that is easily missed by the casual observer. It is a phrase that was spoken by Christ at Bethany after Mary the sister of Lazarus had anointed Him with a very costly perfume. When some objected to the "wasting" of the ointment, Jesus replied: "She hath done what she could."

I'm convinced that our Lord accepted the offering of Fanny Crosby in the same way. Her hymns contain the sweet aroma of her love for Christ. If she had written only this one song, it would have been enough to merit the approval of her Lord.

Blessed assurance, Jesus is mine!
    Oh, what a foretaste of glory divine!
Heir of salvation, purchase of God,
    Born of His Spirit, washed in His blood.

Perfect submission, perfect delight,
    Visions of rapture now burst on my sight;
Angels descending, bring from above
    Echoes of mercy, whispers of love.

Perfect submission, all is at rest,
    I in my Saviour am happy and blest;
Watching and waiting, looking above,
    Filled with His goodness, lost in His love.

Refrain:

This is my story, this is my song,
    Praising my Saviour all the day long;
This is my story, this is my song,
    Praising my Saviour all the day long.

Fanny J. Crosby (1820-1915)

The Son of God goes forth to war,
A kingly crown to gain;
His blood-red banner streams afar:
Who follows in His train?
Who best can drink his cup of woe,
Triumphant over pain,
Who patient bears his cross below,
He follows in His train.

The martyr first, whose eagle eye
Could pierce beyond the grave,
Who saw his Master in the sky,
And called on Him to save:
Like Him, with pardon on his tongue
In midst of mortal pain,
He prayed for them that did the wrong:
Who follows in his train?

A glorious band, the chosen few
On whom the Spirit came,
Twelve valiant saints, their hope they knew,
And mocked the cross and flame:
They met the tyrant's brandished steel,
The lion's gory mane;
They bowed their necks the death to feel:
Who follows in their train?

A noble army, men and boys,
The matron and the maid,
Around the Saviour's throne rejoice,
In robes of light arrayed:
They climbed the steep ascent of heaven
Through peril, toil, and pain;
O God, to us may grace be given
To follow in their train.

Reginald Heber (1783-1826)

the son of God goes forth to war

[*Crusader Hymns*, No. 223]

A Hymn Story by Billy Graham

One of my favorite melodies is the stirring hymn tune named "All Saints, New" which we used with "Macedonia," the theme hymn of the 1966 World Congress on Evangelism in Berlin. The tune was originally written for the text "The Son of God Goes Forth to War," a hymn about Christian martyrs, and that is why it is called "All Saints."
[Read or sing stanzas 1-3.]

The Apostle Paul often spoke of Christian life and service as a warfare. "Put on all the armour which God provides, so that you may be able to stand firm against the devices of the devil. For our fight is not against human foes, but against cosmic powers, against the authorities and potentates of this dark world, against the superhuman forces of evil in the heavens" (Eph. 6:11,12, *New English Bible*). In the verses that follow are listed the pieces of spiritual armor with which we fight this war: the belt of truth, the breastplate of integrity, shoes of the gospel of peace, the shield of faith, the helmet of salvation, and the sword of the Spirit — the Word of God.

In this hymn we see a picture of Jesus Christ at the head of a great battle column. Over and over the question is asked, "Who follows in His train, in His victory procession?" The answer is obvious; Christ's army is made up of men and women who "best can drink their cup of woe" and patiently "bear their cross below."

From the words of the second stanza, we discern that one of the prominent figures in this battle formation is Stephen, the first Christian martyr. Acts chapter seven *(NEB)* tells us that Stephen saw Jesus "standing at God's right hand" and that he prayed for his murderers, "Lord, do not hold this sin against them."

Behind Stephen in the procession, the third stanza mentions "twelve valiant saints," the Lord's twelve apostles. Tradition tells us that they too were martyrs, killed by the sword, by animals in the Roman arena, or by other brutal methods.

And who follows in their train? The hymn writer sees a noble army of "men and boys, the matron and the maid" who down through the years have given their lives for the cause of the gospel of Jesus Christ. Our own century has produced more martyrs than the entire 1900 years since Jesus' death. Included are Dr. Paul Carlson, who died in the Congo uprising of 1964, and the five missionaries murdered by Ecuador's Auca Indians in 1956.

But what kind of an army can this be, following in the train of Jesus Christ? It would seem that they are all casualties of war who lost their lives in battle. Can this be a victorious group?

The Bible records that the brilliant young Jew, Saul of Tarsus, was watching the stoning of Stephen and that the martyr's testimony in death profoundly influenced this persecutor of the church. Soon after, Saul was converted and became Paul the Apostle. Through his missionary journeys and those of all of Jesus' disciples, the gospel was spread throughout the known world and the Christian church was founded.

In our own times, because of the death of Dr. Paul Carlson, a medical foundation has been set up in the Congo; thus his ministry will be multiplied to those who murdered him. And in South America, almost the entire Auca Indian tribe has been won to faith in Jesus Christ as an end result of the death of those five young men. Two of the Aucas — including one who participated in the killing — attended the 1966 Berlin Congress on Evangelism!

I believe that in the days ahead we may experience even greater persecution because of our faith. Many more young men and women may become martyrs for the cause of Christ. Are we willing "to drink the cup which Jesus drank" — the cup of suffering, pain and death? We should remember these words of Paul, who also died a martyr:

> **Take your share of hardship, like a good soldier of Christ Jesus . . . Remember Jesus Christ, risen from the dead, born of David's line. This is the theme of my gospel, in whose service I am exposed to hardship, even to the point of being shut up like a common criminal; but the word of God is not shut up. And I endure it all for the sake of God's chosen ones, with this end in view, that they too may attain the glorious and eternal salvation which is in Christ Jesus.**
>
> **Here are words you may trust: "If we died with him, we shall live with him; if we endure, we shall reign with him" (II Timothy 2:3, 8-12, *NEB*).**

[Read or sing the final stanza.]

SAVED!

[*Crusader Hymns*, No. 110]

The idea that Christians should modernize their speech when talking about their faith is much discussed today. Some of these reactions to traditional language may reveal a bit of cynicism—as for instance the one ridiculing the soul-winner who grabs you by the lapels and says, "Brother, are you saved?"

It must be granted that such a frontal attack may not be the best way to introduce someone to Jesus Christ. We must use an appropriate approach and language that makes sense to our generation. But the word "saved" should be just as intelligible to modern minds as other Biblical words such as "salvation" and "Saviour." After all, this expression appears in some of our most significant scripture passages.

> **For this is good and acceptable in the sight of God our Saviour; who will have all men to be saved, and to come unto the knowledge of the truth (I Tim. 2:3, 4).**
>
> **For whosoever shall call upon the name of the Lord shall be saved (Rom. 10:13).**
>
> **For by grace are ye saved through faith; and that not of yourselves; it is the gift of God: not of works, lest any man should boast (Eph. 2:8, 9).**

The meaning of "saved" is not really obscure. Among other things, it signifies "rescued." We say that a person was "saved from drowning." Similarly, we affirm that through faith in Christ "a soul is saved from eternal loss, judgment and death," and that "a life was saved from frustration and meaninglessness."

The angel of God used this expression in telling Joseph about the son who was to be born to Mary: "Thou shalt call his name Jesus (Saviour); for He shall save His people from their sins." Preachers of the gospel agree that, through the death and resurrection of our Lord, we are "saved from sin" in a threefold way.

First, we are saved, or delivered, from the condemnation and the *penalty* of our sins. Romans 8:1 declares: "There is therefore now no condemnation to them which are in Christ Jesus, who walk not after the flesh, but after the Spirit."

We are also saved, or freed, from the *power* of sin in our lives. This is a progressive freedom. As we walk faithfully with Christ day by day, we experience increasing victory over the temptations and the defeats that are common to men. The Bible has this encouraging promise: "For sin shall not have dominion over you; for ye are not under the law, but under grace" (Rom. 6:14).

Finally, we will one day be saved from the very *presence* of sin. We are told in Revelation 21:27 that "there shall in no wise enter into it (heaven) any thing that defileth." We will also then be freed from all the results of sin. "And God shall wipe away all tears from their eyes; and there shall be no more death, neither sorrow, nor crying, neither shall there be any more pain" (Rev. 21:4).

[Read or sing stanzas 1 and 2.]

The author of this great salvation song is Dr. Oswald J. Smith, for many years pastor of The Peoples Church of Toronto, and one of our outstanding missionary statesmen. Dr. Smith recently wrote:

> **It was in Toronto in 1917, when I was twenty-seven years of age, that I wrote my hymn 'Saved.' At that time I was sending my hymns to the Tabernacle Publishing Company of Chicago. Arthur W. McKee, Paul Rader's great song leader, was the one with whom I corresponded. He sent a number of my hymn-poems to Roger M. Hickman, a Baptist musician and evangelist, and he was the one who wrote the inspiring music.**
>
> **In the year 1919, Dr. Rader and Mr. McKee came to Toronto to hold an evangelistic campaign in Massey Hall. I had just resigned from Dale Presbyterian Church and was out of work. I tried to usher in the meetings but was turned down. I tried to do personal work but was ignored. Then I started selling hymnbooks in the aisles, praying and hoping that God would use me again.**
>
> **Suddenly one night, Mr. McKee announced that they were going to sing a brand new hymn called 'Saved.' My heart was in my mouth. Pointing down to where I was selling hymnbooks McKee said, 'That young man down there wrote this hymn.' I turned my back and went on selling books.**
>
> **Then they sang it — 3400 voices strong — sang it until it seemed as though they would lift the roof. I was hearing it introduced for the first time. Oh, how it stirred me! I had been fearfully discouraged, but that night God spoke to me again and I was inspired and elated. I knew God was not going to put me on the shelf.**
>
> **Then came the Alliance Tabernacle on Christie Street, The Peoples Church and worldwide evangelism. And now, in all parts of the world, and in many languages, for more than fifty years my song has been sung. It is still my testimony, every word of it. May it long live after I am gone, to proclaim the great message of God's salvation.**

[Read or sing the last stanza.]

Saved! saved! saved! my sins are all forgiv'n;
Christ is mine! I'm on my way to heav'n;
Once a guilty sinner, lost, undone,
Now a child of God, saved thro' His Son.

Saved! saved! saved! by grace and grace alone;
Oh, what wondrous love to me was shown,
In my stead Christ Jesus bled and died,
Bore my sins, for me was crucified.

Saved! saved! saved! oh, joy beyond compare!
Christ my life, and I His constant care;
Yielding all and trusting Him alone,
Living now each moment as His own.

Refrain:

Saved! I'm saved thro' Christ, my all in all;
Saved! I'm saved, whatever may befall;
He died upon the cross for me, He bore the awful penalty;
And now I'm saved eternally — I'm saved! saved! saved!

Oswald J. Smith (b. 1890)

And can it be that I should gain
        An interest in the Saviour's blood?
Died He for me, who caused His pain?
        For me, who Him to death pursued?
Amazing love! how can it be
        That Thou, my God, shouldst die for me?

'Tis mystery all! Th'Immortal dies!
        Who can explore His strange design?
In vain the first-born seraph tries
        To sound the depths of love Divine!
'Tis mercy all! let earth adore,
        Let angel minds inquire no more.

He left His Father's throne above,
        So free, so infinite His grace;
Emptied Himself of all but love,
        And bled for Adam's helpless race;
'Tis mercy all, immense and free;
        For, O my God, it found out me.

Long my imprisoned spirit lay
        Fast bound in sin and nature's night;
Thine eye diffused a quick'ning ray,
        I woke, the dungeon flamed with light;
My chains fell off, my heart was free;
        I rose, went forth, and followed Thee.

No condemnation now I dread;
        Jesus, and all in Him, is mine!
Alive in Him, my living Head,
        And clothed in righteousness Divine,
Bold I approach th'eternal throne,
        And claim the crown, thro' Christ my own.

Charles Wesley (1707-1788)

And Can It Be That I Should Gain?

[*Crusader Hymns,* No. 74]

A Hymn Story by Cliff Barrows

One of the most gripping songs about salvation in all hymnody is "And Can it Be;" it is especially strong when sung to the thrilling tune "Sagina." The poem presents the drama of man's redemption in two parts: first, the Lord's sacrifice to provide our salvation; and second, our experience when we accept His offering for us.
[Read or sing stanzas 1-3.]

Not many hymns begin with a question as does this one. However, it is not an expression of doubt but of wonder and awe. How can it be that the shedding of Jesus' blood 1900 years ago is relevant to me today? How was it possible for the Son of God to have died for me? Why should our Lord empty Himself of all His divine glory and become a man, in order to save "Adam's helpless race?" It is said in stanza two that even the angels—including Gabriel, who is called the "first-born seraph" —try in vain to understand.

Charles Wesley, author of this hymn, may have been thinking of the earlier words of Isaac Watts:

Alas, and did my Saviour bleed?
And did my Sovereign die?
Would He devote that sacred head
For such a worm as I?

Watts' attempt to explain the mystery is also limited to an expression of wonder: "Amazing pity! grace unknown! and love beyond degree!"

It is Wesley's advice that we do not waste time in a fruitless attempt to understand in full. It is beyond the comprehension of angels. Let us simply accept the fact of God's love, and then lift our hearts in adoration to Christ.

This is the mystery of Christ's death. What does it mean in the experience of the individual believer?
[Read or sing stanzas 4 and 5.]

There is considerable evidence that this hymn was written by Charles Wesley soon after his own conversion. Looking back, he sees himself as a prisoner in a dark dungeon, chained by the *sins* which he had committed and even more made captive by the *sin* which was a part of his very nature. The gospel of Christ—the good news that Christ had died to meet his need—seemed to flood the dungeon with light, break the chains, and set him free. His feeling of guilt was gone. For the first time he seemed to be really alive, because he possessed the supernatural life of Jesus Christ! He could face the final judgment unafraid because he was clothed in the very righteousness of Christ.

It may sound as if this were the dramatic experience of one who was rescued from a life of terrible sin and degradation. But, at the time of his conversion, Charles Wesley had already been a rector in the Church of England for three years; he had just returned from a term as missionary to Georgia in the New World. Even before that, he and his brother John had earned the derisive name "Methodist" because of the disciplined life which they imposed on themselves and other members of the "Holy Club" at Oxford University. But, in all this religious activity, he had never found spiritual peace; he was not convinced that the life of Christ was really his!

When our evangelistic crusades are held in London, we often drive past the location on Aldersgate street where history says that the Wesleys found Christian assurance for themselves. Nearby is the Wesley home and the chapel they built for worship.

Charles Wesley's crisis experience occurred on May 20, 1738. He had been sick in body as well as in spirit. It seemed that God spoke to him through a vision. According to his *Journal*, this confrontation took place after reading the Bible for some time. Following is his account:

> **At midnight I gave myself up to Christ: assured I was safe, sleeping or waking. Had continued experience of his power to overcome all temptations; and confessed, with joy and surprise, that he was able to do exceedingly abundantly for me, above what I can ask or think.**

Nineteen hundred years ago, when Jesus said to Nicodemus, "Ye must be born again," he was talking to one of the leaders of the Jewish community, one of the most respected men of that day. I recently heard of a seventy-one-year-old minister who, after spending fifty years in the service of the church, had just come to know Jesus Christ as his Saviour.

Like the experience Charles Wesley describes in this hymn, the old minister learned personally to know God. He realized as we must also, that "doing good" means nothing to God. To accept Christ's love and sacrifice for himself was to find the source of the Christian life.

[Read or sing stanza 1 again.]

Lord, I have shut the door

[*Crusader Hymns*, No. 164]

A Hymn Story by Don Hustad

[Read or sing stanza 1.]

And now about prayer. When you pray, don't be like the hypocrites who pretend piety by praying publicly on street corners and in the synagogues where everyone can see them! Truly, that is all the reward they will ever get! But when you pray, go away by yourself, all alone, and shut the door behind you and pray to your Father secretly, and your Father, who knows your secrets, will reward you (Matthew 6:5,6, *Living Gospels*).

Here's a good question to ask ourselves. Are we ever guilty of praying horizontally — for people, instead of vertically — to God? When we lead in prayer at home or in church, are we too concerned about the impression we are making on other people? Well, even if we do not indulge in "show off" prayer, this is still good advice: "When you pray, go away by yourself, all alone."

I must admit that this is very difficult for me to do nowadays. From the moment a day begins in our home, life is a bustle of activity: getting the girls off to school, answering the telephone, rushing to the airport, going to crusade meetings or to our own church, entertaining our friends, and keeping up with music practice and correspondence.

Even on the rare occasions when families are at home today, they are seldom really quiet. The noise of traffic, of jet airplanes, of telephone and television, of hi-fi phonographs and transistor radios bores in upon them. Someone has said that the hearing capacity as well as the spiritual tone of the present generation is bound to be harmed by the "high decibel" rate of life as we know it.

It may be that modern man doesn't really want to be quiet, because then he is forced into sober and serious thinking. He hides from his inner fears, his weaknesses and failures, by constant talking and doing. If he commits some sin — if he says an unkind word or thinks an evil thought — he shuts it out of his mind by rushing to some new task or to another chat on the telephone. We need often to "shut the door" and pray, in order that we might really know ourselves and understand our deepest problems.

It is also true that unless we pray in this manner prescribed by our Lord, we do not really find God! Do you remember the story of Elijah's flight from King Ahab and Queen Jezebel? He was on the mountain called Horeb waiting to hear from God. I Kings 19:11, 12 says that:

> **a great and strong wind rent the mountains, and brake in pieces the rocks before the Lord; but the Lord was not in the wind; and after the wind an earthquake; but the Lord was not in the earthquake: and after the earthquake a fire; but the Lord was not in the fire: and after the fire a still small voice.**

God is not going to shout at us over the noise and the busy-ness of our lives. His voice is a quiet one, but it can be heard if we follow the Psalmist's advice: "Be still, and know that I am God" (Psalm 46:10).

Every individual must solve for himself this problem of securing privacy so that he can think and pray. It may be that in your home, only the basement is out of the main stream of traffic. My wife complains that the children are always bursting in with some problem about clothes or dates, even into her bedroom at night. Some people find they can pray best in the early morning, before the telephone, radio and TV get into gear. Others can do it while riding the train or bus to work. (If you obey the command "watch and pray" in an ultra-literal sense, you may also commune with God while you're driving.) You can even pray while walking your dog late in the evening! However you or I work it out, every one of us needs to shut the door on our busy world if we are to really pray.

William M. Runyan, author of both words and music of this hymn, was the kind of person who had evidently learned this secret. I remember him as a charming, friendly man of great dignity who occasionally dropped in at the Moody Bible Institute while he was editing hymnals for the Hope Publishing Company. Earlier in life he had been a Methodist pastor and evangelist.

Our last visit together was during his retirement in Galveston, Texas, when the Moody Chorale sang there. His very manner and his conversation revealed that, although he knew much about the world in which he lived, his greater acquaintance with God had given him a serenity which is rare in these hectic days. The dynamic for personal poise and power in meeting life's problems is found in these words of scripture: "Go away by yourself, all alone, and shut the door behind you and pray to your Father secretly, and your Father, who knows your secrets, will reward you."

[Read or sing stanzas 2-4.]

Lord, I have shut the door; speak now the word
Which in the din and throng could not be heard;
Hushed now my inner heart, whisper Thy will,
While I have come apart, while all is still.

Lord, I have shut the door, here do I bow;
Speak, for my soul attent turns to Thee now.
Rebuke Thou what is vain, counsel my soul,
Thy holy will reveal, my will control.

In this blest quietness clamorings cease;
Here in Thy presence dwells infinite peace;
Yonder the strife and cry, yonder the sin:
Lord, I have shut the door, Thou art within!

Lord, I have shut the door, strengthen my heart;
Yonder awaits the task — I share a part,
Only through grace bestowed may I be true;
Here, while alone with Thee, my strength renew.

William M. Runyan (1870-1957)

Free from the law, O happy condition,
Jesus hath bled, and there is remission;
Cursed by the law and bruised by the fall,
Grace hath redeemed us once for all.

Now are we free — there's no condemnation,
Jesus provides a perfect salvation;
"Come unto Me," O hear His sweet call,
Come, and He saves us once for all.

"Children of God," O glorious calling,
Surely His grace will keep us from falling;
Passing from death to life at His call,
Blessed salvation once for all.

Refrain:

Once for all, O sinner, receive it;
Once for all, O brother, believe it;
Cling to the cross, the burden will fall,
Christ hath redeemed us once for all.

Philip P. Bliss (1838-1876)

Once for All

[*Crusader Hymns,* No. 119]

A Hymn Story by Billy Graham

While we were ministering in Edinburgh, Scotland in 1955, our Association was able to give some financial assistance to the famous Carruber's Close Mission which was founded by D. L. Moody many years ago. In appreciation, the mission leaders helped us acquire the reed organ which had been used by the gospel singer Ira D. Sankey when he and Moody worked together in Great Britain. The little organ has been preserved and is now exhibited in our offices in Minneapolis, Minnesota.

Every time I see it there, I am reminded of Sankey's first appearance in Edinburgh. The Presbyterians in Scotland had long insisted that only the "psalms" should be sung in church, and these without any accompaniment. On an earlier occasion, one lady had walked out on a Moody-Sankey meeting, protesting that the devil was in his "kist (chest) o' whistles." Sankey's concern about the Scots' acceptance of his simple "gospel hymns" was increased when he saw the great preacher and hymnwriter Horatius Bonar in the audience. As he recounts it, this is the narrative from *My Life and the Story of the Gospel Hymns:*

> **Of all men in Scotland he was the one concerning whose decision I was most solicitous. He was, indeed, my ideal hymn writer, the prince among hymnists of his day and generation. And yet he would not sing one of his beautiful hymns in his own congregation . . . because he ministered to a church that believed in the use of the Psalms only.**
>
> **With fear and trembling I announced as a solo the song, 'Free from the Law, oh, happy condition.' . . . Feeling that the singing might prove only an entertainment and not a spiritual blessing, I requested the whole congregation to join me in a word of prayer, asking God to bless the truth about to be sung. In the prayer my anxiety was relieved. Believing and rejoicing in the glorious truth contained in the song, I sang it through to the end.**
>
> **At the close of Mr. Moody's address, Dr. Bonar turned toward me with a smile on his venerable face, and reaching out his hand he said: "Well, Mr. Sankey, you sang the gospel tonight." And thus the way was opened for the mission of sacred song in Scotland.**

The choice of song Ira Sankey made that night had truly been dictated by God's leading. Its statement of faith included the whole story of sin and death, of grace and salvation. What better appeal could be made to a people who prided themselves on their doctrinal scholarship!

This simple hymn contains the basis of our Christian theology, from the fall of man to his final redemption in heaven. The Bible says that the Devil, in the form of a serpent, tempted the first man and caused him to sin, to fall from his state of perfect fellowship with God. Genesis 3:15 teaches that Satan "bruised the heel" of man in this act. When the created being thus became estranged from his Creator, determined to work out his own destiny, God gave a set of laws to show that man cannot please Him in his own strength; neither can he find complete happiness in himself or in his relationships with other men.

The penalty for breaking God's law is death, as is stated in Romans 6:23: "For the wages of sin is death." Furthermore, God knew that nobody could keep the law perfectly; this failure must ultimately pass a death sentence on the entire human race. This universal judgment is confirmed in Galatians 3:10: "Cursed is every one that continueth not in *all* things which are written in the book of the law to do them."

In His great wisdom and because of His great love, God provided that His Son Jesus Christ would bear our penalty and make possible the restoration of fellowship. Now we are "free from the law of sin and death" (Rom. 8:2). Galatians 3:13 says that "Christ hath redeemed us from the curse of the law."

The title of this hymn comes from Hebrews 10:10, "By the which will we are sanctified (set apart, made holy) through the offering of the body of Jesus Christ *once for all.*" Jesus died on Calvary almost two thousand years ago, but His death provides salvation for all who have believed in Him, and for all who will believe in the years to come.

When we accept Christ's sacrifice for us, there is "no more condemnation." God forgives all our sins, and by so doing frees our consciences from a sense of guilt. The Bible testifies that then "the Spirit itself beareth witness with our spirit, that we are the children of God" (Rom. 8:16). We have "passed from death unto life" (John 5:24). In addition, we are given the promise that Christ will keep us from falling into sin again if we walk day by day as His Word teaches us. "Now unto him that is able to keep you from falling, and to present you faultless before the presence of his glory with exceeding joy; to the only wise God our Saviour, be glory and majesty, dominion and power, both now and ever. Amen." (Jude 24, 25)

All this information is contained in the gospel song "Once For All." This hymn is almost a century old, but its message is timeless. It is just as relevant today as the scriptures upon which it is based.

[Read or sing the entire hymn.]

holy spirit, breathe on me

[*Crusader Hymns*, No. 176]

A Hymn Story by Cliff Barrows

Both because of his size and accomplishment, B. B. McKinney stood out as a giant in the field of gospel music during the early twentieth century. McKinney was a big man—more than six feet tall and two hundred pounds in weight—with a large, warm-hearted personality to match. He was both a winsome and commanding figure, whether he was singing a solo, directing an evangelistic choir, or managing an office.

His contributions to the Southern Baptist ministry accorded him a title as "the father of church music among Southern Baptists." After teaching at Southwestern Seminary and serving as assistant pastor of the Travis Avenue Baptist Church in Fort Worth, Texas, he became secretary of the newly-organized Church Music Department at Baptist headquarters in Nashville, Tennessee. Here he edited the first hymnals to be widely used by Southern Baptists, and initiated the now-burgeoning ministry in church music.

Besides this educational ministry, he exercised a personal talent for composing. Among the 150 songs for which Dr. McKinney wrote both words and music, there are at least two which are adaptations of earlier hymns by other writers. One of these, "Holy Spirit, Breathe on Me" gives us McKinney's personal understanding of the hymn "Breathe on Me, Breath of God." The original was written in 1878 by Edwin Hatch, a professor at Oxford University.

Borrowing from earlier hymnic sources, as McKinney did in this instance, is a fairly common practice. Many of Isaac Watts' hymns are adaptations of the Jewish hymns we call "psalms;" for instance, "O God, Our Help in Ages Past" (Number 12, *Crusader Hymns*) is based on Psalm 90. Similarly, "Just As I Am, Thine Own to Be" (Number 66) is a youth version of "Just As I Am, Without One Plea" (Number 57). J. Wilbur Chapman's "Our Great Saviour" (Number 4) quotes many phrases from Charles Wesley's "Jesus, Lover of My Soul" (Number 79). I believe it should be regarded as a compliment to the earlier hymn when a subsequent writer wants to re-state its truth in his own words.

At first glance, both these titles, "Holy Spirit, Breathe on Me" and "Breathe on Me, Breath of God," may seem a bit odd. To personify and address diety so directly may appear presumptuous. However, in the original language of the New Testament the word for "spirit" is *pneuma*, which means "wind" or "breath." On the day of Pentecost, the Holy Spirit's coming was accompanied with "a sound from heaven as of a rushing mighty wind" (Acts 2:2). In anticipation of that day, John 20:22 *(Living Gospels)* says that Jesus "breathed" on his disciples and said, "Receive the Holy Spirit."

The verses of this hymn tell what the Holy Spirit does for the Christian, because He dwells in the believer's heart. The words "Breathe on me, until my heart is clean" in stanza one, remind us that it is God's Spirit who daily cleanses or "sanctifies" us, causing us to be more and more like Jesus Christ. Paul said to the Corinthians: "But ye are washed, but ye are sanctified, but ye are justified in the name of the Lord Jesus, and by the Spirit of our God" (I Cor. 6:11).

[Read or sing stanza 1.]

It is the Holy Spirit who also leads us to consecrate ourselves to Christ. "Holy Spirit, breathe on me, My stubborn will subdue," the stanzas continue. In the scriptures, Ephesians 5:18 reiterates this in another way, "And be not drunk with wine, wherein is excess; but be filled with the Spirit." A man who is under the influence of intoxicants does not have control over his own actions; he is dominated by the effects of the alcohol. When we are filled with the Holy Spirit we are under His complete control to do the perfect will of God.

[Read or sing stanza 2.]

The third stanza states that it is the Holy Spirit who gives us spiritual power to become mature personalities capable of serving God more effectively. So we sing in a spirit of prayer, "Holy Spirit, breathe on me, Fill me with pow'r divine." Christ promised his disciples, "Ye shall receive power, after that the Holy Ghost is come upon you: and ye shall be witnesses unto me." It was this power that enabled the early Christians to spread the gospel throughout the known world within their lifetimes. The same resource for effective ministry is available today.

As we live each day, the Holy Spirit wants to do these same things for us, and in the same order. First, He would cleanse us from sin; second, He wants to help us dedicate ourselves completely to God; and finally, He desires to give us all the resources of God so that we may live triumphantly.

[Read or sing stanzas 3 and 4.]

Holy Spirit, breathe on me
Until my heart is clean;
Let sunshine fill its inmost part,
With not a cloud between.

Holy Spirit, breathe on me,
My stubborn will subdue;
Teach me in words of living flame
What Christ would have me do.

Holy Spirit, breathe on me,
Fill me with pow'r divine;
Kindle a flame of love and zeal
Within this heart of mine.

Holy Spirit, breathe on me,
Till I am all Thine own;
Until my will is lost in Thine,
To live for Thee alone.

Refrain:

Breathe on me, breathe on me,
Holy Spirit, breathe on me;
Take Thou my heart, cleanse every part,
Holy Spirit, breathe on me.

Edwin Hatch (1835-1889)
Alt. by B. B. McKinney (1886-1952)

Thy Word is like a garden, Lord,
With flowers bright and fair;
And every one who seeks may pluck
A lovely cluster there.
Thy Word is like a deep, deep mine;
And jewels rich and rare
Are hidden in its mighty depths
For every searcher there.

Thy Word is like a starry host:
A thousand rays of light
Are seen to guide the traveler,
And make his pathway bright.
Thy Word is like an armory,
Where soldiers may repair,
And find, for life's long battle-day,
All needful weapons there.

O may I love Thy precious Word,
May I explore the mine,
May I its fragrant flowers glean,
May light upon me shine.
O may I find my armor there,
Thy Word my trusty sword;
I'll learn to fight with every foe
The battle of the Lord.

Edwin Hodder (1837-1904)

Thy Word Is Like a Garden, Lord

[*Crusader Hymns*, No. 204]

The Bible is an amazing book! Although parts of it are almost three thousand years old, it has for years been the world's best-seller, and it is constantly being translated into new languages. Throughout two centuries of "higher criticism" the scriptures have been under constant attack because of a few apparent discrepancies. Yet, apart from God, its unity is unexplainable, since it was penned in three different languages, by more than forty different individuals, over a period of a thousand years. Each year the archeologist's shovel confirms more of what the Bible has recorded about human history.

Unlike any other volume in the world's libraries, the Bible is a miracle book — the living Word of God. It has altered the patterns of society and changed the destiny of nations. It has transformed individual lives. This hymn tells us why this is so.

"Thy Word is like a garden, Lord" suggests first that the Bible is comparable to a landscape full of lovely flowers that bring delight with every glance. We pick up a paraphrase like *Living Gospels* or J. B. Phillips' *Letters to Young Churches* and read it easily like a novel, with both pleasure and profit. Most public gardens have signs posted which warn: "Please do not pick the flowers." But in the garden of God's Word we read "Help yourself!"

Richard Cecil, in his book *Remains*, uses this same idea to say that every word in the Bible is important. "The Bible resembles an extensive garden, where there is a vast variety and profusion of fruits and flowers, some of which are more essential or more splendid than others; but there is not a blade suffered to grow in it which has not its use and beauty in the system."

The Bible is also like "a deep, deep mine" containing priceless jewels. These treasures may not be picked up in a casual stroll through the garden. They require digging — long and careful study — and perhaps some mining tools, such as different versions, dictionaries and commentaries. But we will find that both the predictable and the unexpected prizes we turn up are well worth all the hard work required. As the late Dr. M. R. De Haan of the "Radio Bible Class" once said, "The 'fringe benefits' of Bible study may be more precious than the thing we started looking for originally."

Psalm 119:105 declares that the scriptures are like a lantern: "Thy word is a lamp unto my feet, and a light unto my path." Our hymn carries the analogy a little further and says that the Bible is like the star-filled heavens, lighting up the entire landscape. Navigators use the celestial bodies to secure a "compass fix" and to chart the route of a great ship or an airliner. So God's Word gives direction to the whole course of our life and lights each step we take.

Finally, the Bible is like an armory in which are stored all kinds of weapons for the warfare against sin and the devil. When Jesus was tempted in the wilderness by Satan, He used the scriptures to repel the subtle, insidious assaults of the wicked one. If we memorize passages from the Word of God, they will become ever-ready weapons of defense whenever we are threatened by evil thoughts and desires.

Ephesians 6:17 states that God's Word is also an offensive weapon — "the sword of the Spirit." When we would win a victory in our own character development or in doing the work of Christ here on earth, it is the Bible which strengthens us and makes it possible.

The Bible is all this and more, according to the testimony of some of the world's greatest men:

Immanuel Kant — "The Bible is the greatest benefit which the human race has ever experienced."

Abraham Lincoln — "Read this book for what on reason you can accept and take the rest on faith, and you will live and die a better man."

John Ruskin — "The Bible is the one Book to which any thoughtful man may go with any honest question of life or destiny and find the answer of God by honest searching."

[Read or sing the entire hymn.]

Some of our hymn writers were neither ministers nor professional poets, but ordinary people who loved to sing and to write new Christian songs. Edwin Hodder (1837-1904), author of "Thy Word Is Like a Garden, Lord," spent the early part of his working life in New Zealand, doing sociological research among the Maori aborigines. Later he became a civil servant in his native England. As a hymnist, he would probably be called an amateur, but in this hymn alone he has made a great contribution to our worship.

all my life long

[*Crusader Hymns*, No. 107]

A Hymn Story by George Beverly Shea

When I was a boy of eight our family moved from Winchester, Ontario to Houghton, New York. My father had been a pastor in Winchester for twenty years and was now beginning a brief period of ministry in evangelism and church pioneering.

Walking together in Houghton one day, Dad pointed out a tall, elderly lady moving slowly along the sidewalk. He told me that she was Mrs. Clara Tear Williams, a much loved and respected hymn writer — author of one of his favorite Christian songs, "Satisfied." From that time on, Mrs. Williams' appearance always reminded me of the classic painting of Whistler's mother. She had a regal and dignified bearing and yet she had the kindness and gentleness of Christ in her face. When I came to know her and often spoke with her, I enjoyed the soft, musical tones of her voice. Through her sweetness and graciousness to everyone, she became another wonderful proof to me of the reality of the Christian walk. Hers was a beautiful life exhibited not only to the whole community, but expressed also in the pages of hymnody.

Some time afterward I memorized this hymn. It became one of my first solos as I began to sing publicly in my late teens. At that time my father had a pastorate in Ottawa, Canada. Since then I have always loved to sing it because "All My Life Long" expresses the conviction of everyone who has found satisfaction in Jesus Christ.

Like my family, Mrs. Williams was a Wesleyan Methodist. The composer of the hymn's melody, Ralph E. Hudson, was associated with the older Methodist Episcopal Church. After serving as a male nurse during the Civil War, he became a music teacher and publisher in Ohio. He was often engaged as an evangelistic singer, and wrote many gospel hymn tunes.

[Read or sing stanzas 1 and 2.]

Clara Williams' hymn is as modern as the concerns of mankind. Psychologists today refer to a person's fundamental needs — a need for security, a need to be loved, and a need to find identity. In this hymn these inner longings are represented by metaphors of hunger, thirst and a desire for material riches. Many men and women pursue these elemental physical wants, thinking that they will meet their deeper needs. But, of course, they never do.

Others expect that happiness will result from gratifying the desires of the mind and the ego. A thirst for knowledge and a hunger for power characterizes many men, accompanied by a desire for status and recognition. But these ambitions, too, finally become futile; as the hymn says, they are only "dust which we gather around us."

King Solomon exemplified a person who relentlessly pursued satisfaction in many areas. As a young man, he enjoyed everything that could please the body: rich foods, exotic wines, and other sensual pleasures.

When he became king of Israel, Solomon experienced great power and glory. He was a connoisseur of the arts and built one of the world's most beautiful temples. He displayed great wisdom in his judgments and even practiced religion — but without true faith in God.

At the end of life, Solomon looked back over his long and fruitless quest for happiness, and exclaimed, "Vanity, vanity, all is vanity!"

The final stanza of our hymn says that Jesus Christ alone can meet the deepest longings of men. He becomes to us a "well of water," the "bread of life," and "untold wealth that never faileth." Recall these words spoken by Jesus himself:

> **"If any man thirst, let him come unto me, and drink" (John 7:37).**
>
> **"I am the bread of life: he that cometh to me shall never hunger; and he that believeth on me shall never thirst" (John 6:35).**
>
> **"Seek ye first the kingdom of God, and his righteousness; and all these things shall be added unto you" (Matt. 6:33).**

The truth is, no man can ever find true happiness apart from Jesus Christ. As St. Augustine said in his prayer, long ago, "Thou hast created us for Thyself, and our heart cannot be quieted till it find repose in Thee."

[Read or sing stanzas 3 and 4.]

All my life long I had panted
        For a drink from some cool spring
That I hoped would quench the burning
        Of the thirst I felt within.

Feeding on the husks around me
        Till my strength was almost gone,
Longed my soul for something better,
        Only still to hunger on.

Poor I was, and sought for riches,
        Something that would satisfy;
But the dust I gathered round me
        Only mocked my soul's sad cry.

Well of water, ever springing,
        Bread of life, so rich and free,
Untold wealth that never faileth,
        My Redeemer is to me.

Refrain:

Hallelujah! I have found Him —
        Whom my soul so long has craved!
Jesus satisfies my longings;
        Thro' His blood I now am saved.

Clara Tear Williams (1858-1937)

How firm a foundation, ye saints of the Lord,
Is laid for your faith in His excellent Word;
What more can He say than to you He hath said,
To you who for refuge to Jesus have fled?

"Fear not, I am with thee; O be not dismayed,
For I am thy God, and will still give thee aid;
I'll strengthen thee, help thee, and cause thee to stand,
Upheld by my righteous, omnipotent hand.

"When through fiery trials thy pathway shall lie,
My grace, all sufficient, shall be thy supply;
The flame shall not hurt thee; I only design
Thy dross to consume, and thy gold to refine.

"The soul that on Jesus hath leaned for repose,
I will not, I will not desert to his foes;
That soul, though all hell should endeavor to shake,
I'll never, no, never, no, never forsake!"

K. in Rippon's
A Selection of Hymns, 1787; Alt.

How Firm a Foundation

[*Crusader Hymns,* No. 180]

When he left the presidency, Andrew Jackson retired to his famous home, the Hermitage, where his many friends often came to visit — the world's great from afar as well as his simple neighbors nearby. On one such occasion, General Jackson said to a local clergyman: "There is a beautiful hymn on the subject of the exceeding great and precious promises of God to His people. It was a favorite hymn with my dear wife till the day of her death. It commences thus: 'How firm a foundation, ye saints of the Lord!' I wish you would sing it now." And so, to please the ex-president, the visitors sang the entire seven stanzas.

Although this hymn has been a favorite in America ever since it appeared in 1787, its authorship is unknown. When first published by Dr. John Rippon, a Baptist minister in London, it was signed simply "K — ", and efforts to identify "K — " with certainty have been fruitless. The tune called "Foundation" has also been credited to various individuals, but without proof we can only call it an "American folk melody."

Andrew Jackson's request revealed that he knew the Bible as well as the hymn. When these verses first appeared, they bore the scripture text: "Whereby are given unto us exceeding great and precious promises" (II Peter 1:4). The hymnwriter sets forth his entire message in the first lines; God's Word, the Bible, tells us that our faith in God is not misplaced. We have been assured, in the words of Moses to the children of Israel: "Be strong and of a good courage, fear not . . . for the Lord thy God, he it is that doth go with thee; he will not fail thee, nor forsake thee" (Deut. 31:6).

This particular promise appears several times in scripture, in almost these same words. God first said it to Abraham (Gen. 28:15) and later to Moses (Deut. 31:8) and then to Joshua (Josh. 1:5). King David repeated the promise to his son Solomon (I Chron. 28:20). As the songwriter asks: What more can God say?

The second stanza is taken directly from Isaiah 41:10, "Fear thou not, for I am with thee: be not dismayed, for I am thy God; I will strengthen thee; yea, I will help thee; yea, I will uphold thee with the right hand of my righteousness."

[Read or sing stanzas 1 and 2.]

A stanza of "How Firm a Foundation" that is not always included in hymnals reads this way:

> When through the deep water I call thee to go,
> The rivers of sorrow shall not overflow;
> For I will be with thee thy trials to bless,
> And sanctify to thee thy deepest distress.

These words, and those of the third stanza included here, come from Isaiah 43:2, "When thou passest through the waters, I will be with thee; and through the rivers, they shall not overflow thee: when thou walkest through the fire, thou shalt not be burned; neither shall the flame kindle upon thee."

Some people have the mistaken notion that a Christian is somehow free from trouble and sorrow. A few of our gospel songs may seem to give that impression, in such phrases as "Every burden of my heart rolled away" or "Jesus took my burdens all away." What these songs mean to say is that the oppressive load of sin and guilt is gone when we know Christ personally as Saviour.

But the ordinary problems and tragedies that are a part of mortal existence do not bypass the believer. In fact, he may often seem to have even more than his share, for these trials perform a special function in his life. Paul said in Romans 5:3,4: "Tribulation (or pressures) worketh patience, and patience, experience; and experience, hope." Our song declares that God uses these difficult experiences to help us become full-orbed Christians—with the "dross of our lives burned away, and the gold refined."

In the Billy Graham motion picture "For Pete's Sake," the young minister says to Pete, when his world seemed to come crashing down around him, "Christ has promised you nothing – nothing but Himself!" And that is enough! For He is with us in all the experiences of life, and that is what makes all the difference.

[Read or sing stanzas 3 and 4.]

A missionary, Fidelia Fisk, was in feeble health, with aching head and tired body, and very much discouraged. The woes of life pressed upon her like a great burden and she was about to sink beneath them. Seeing her depression, a native woman came and sat down behind her on the mat and whispered, "Lean on me." Miss Fisk, unheeding, still longed for assistance in bearing her burden. Presently came again the insistent "Lean on me." This time she leaned gently, but that did not satisfy her pleading friend. In most earnest tones the voice urged again, "If you love me, lean harder."

Everyone at times is weighed down with a particular load of trouble, disappointment or sorrow. To each of us, in times like these, the final stanza of our hymn says, "Lean hard on Jesus Christ."

O Beautiful for Spacious Skies

[*Crusader Hymns,* No. 283]

A Hymn Story by Billy Graham

[Read or sing stanza 1.]

On a summer day in 1893 Katharine Lee Bates, renowned author and professor of English at Wellesley College, stood on Pike's Peak in Colorado. On three sides of her – north, west and south – stretched the majestic rocky mountains dressed in the purple haze which is common to the western United States. To the east was the fruitful Colorado plain, and just beyond the amber-colored grain fields of Kansas and Nebraska.

As she stood on the windy mountain top, Miss Bates imagined she could see the settlers who had trekked across those grasslands decades earlier to find new homes and new opportunities in the west. She remembered also the pilgrims who had first come to America's shores, expecting and finding a new life of freedom.

She thought as well of those who had laid down their lives for their country in the Revolutionary and Civil Wars, because they loved freedom and mercy more than life itself. This was her beloved country – America the Beautiful – beautiful in nature's gifts and in the dedication of those who had been part of its history.

As Katharine Bates returned to her hotel in Colorado Springs, a poem began to take shape in her mind and she began to put it on paper. She recalled also that, on her trip west, she had visited the Columbian Exposition on Chicago's south side. There an "alabaster city" of classic beauty had been erected to show what America's "cities of the future" should be like. She closed her hymn with a prayer that our cities may be as beautiful as the landscape God has prepared for them.

[Read or sing stanzas 2-4.]

Throughout the hymn, with all of her gratitude and admiration for America, Katharine Bates shows that she is very much aware of our weaknesses. During the last part of her life, she began to see the social reforms which gave us our child-labor laws, anti-trust legislation, nation-wide education and universal suffrage. And yet our country has much to desire!

Today we have the highest standard of living in the world – but also the highest crime rate, the highest rate of divorce, the highest rate of suicide. We spend far more each year for liquor, tobacco and gambling than we do for all the work of the church, both at home and abroad.

Sometimes we wonder why our forefathers were so slow to recognize the sin of slavery, yet we are even slower to help the negro emerge from the poverty, ignorance and degradation into which he was forced against his own will. We may point the finger of scorn at the monopolists of yesterday, but we too are bowing to the god of gold in our own day, and at the same time piling up a staggering national debt. It is sobering to learn that the site of the beautiful 1893 Columbian Exposition is now adjacent to one of our country's worst ghettos!

This great national hymn has occasionally been criticized. It is said that the bland prayer "God shed His grace on thee" fails to recognize our individual spiritual responsibility under God. However, I believe Katharine Bates remembered that the star of hope which led the first pilgrims was a desire to worship God and serve Him in freedom. In terms of material prosperity and personal freedom, no nation in history has been blessed more than our own. I believe that this is true because America was established as a "nation under God" — with Christian faith as the cornerstone of liberty.

Today our nation is threatened as never before — threatened by enemies without, but especially by decadence within. In our day, there seem to be many who believe that "freedom of worship" means freedom *from* worship. If we are to survive as a great country — if we are to achieve brotherhood, self-control and "liberty in law" — we must return to the faith on which America was founded. God will again shed His grace on America, if we will turn to Him in repentance.

Willis Haymaker, a friend and associate through much of my ministry, often uses a certain scripture passage in challenging a city to prepare for an evangelistic crusade. I believe it is appropriate for all America.

> **If my people, which are called by my name, shall humble themselves, and pray, and seek my face, and turn from their wicked ways; then will I hear from heaven, and will forgive their sin, and will heal their land (II Chron. 7:14).**

O beautiful for spacious skies,
For amber waves of grain,
For purple mountain majesties
Above the fruited plain!
America! America!
God shed His grace on thee,
And crown thy good with brotherhood
From sea to shining sea!

O beautiful for pilgrim feet,
Whose stern, impassioned stress
A thoroughfare for freedom beat
Across the wilderness!
America! America!
God mend thine every flaw,
Confirm thy soul in self-control,
Thy liberty in law!

O beautiful for heroes proved
In liberating strife,
Who more than self their country loved,
And mercy more than life!
America! America!
May God thy gold refine
Till all success be nobleness
And every gain divine!

O beautiful for patriot dream
That sees beyond the years
Thine alabaster cities gleam,
Undimmed by human tears!
America! America!
God shed His grace on thee,
And crown thy good with brotherhood
From sea to shining sea!

Katharine Lee Bates (1859-1929)

Brightly beams our Father's mercy
From His lighthouse evermore,
But to us He gives the keeping
Of the lights along the shore.

Dark the night of sin has settled,
Loud the angry billows roar;
Eager eyes are watching, longing,
For the lights along the shore.

Trim your feeble lamp, my brother;
Some poor sailor tempest-tossed,
Trying now to make the harbor,
In the darkness may be lost.

Refrain:

Let the lower lights be burning!
Send a gleam across the wave!
Some poor fainting, struggling seaman
You may rescue, you may save.

Philip P. Bliss (1838-1876)

Let the Lower Lights Be Burning

[*Crusader Hymns,* No. 233]

A Hymn Story by Billy Graham

D. L. Moody, the great evangelist of the last century, often told this story to illustrate each Christian's responsibility to point others to our Lord.

> **On a dark, stormy night when the waves rolled like mountains and not a star could be seen, a large passenger boat cautiously edged toward the Cleveland harbor. The pilot knew that, in the inky darkness, he could only find the harbor channel by keeping two lower shore lights in line with the main beacon.**
>
> **"Are you sure this is Cleveland?" asked the captain, seeing only one light from the lighthouse.**
>
> **"Quite sure, sir," replied the pilot.**
>
> **"Where are the lower lights?" he asked.**
>
> **"Gone out, sir," was the reply.**
>
> **"Can you make the harbor?"**
>
> **"We must or perish, sir!"**
>
> **With a strong hand and a brave heart, the old pilot turned the wheel. But alas! In the darkness he missed the channel, the boat crashed on the rocks, and many lives were lost.**

D. L. Moody's closing words were: "Brethren, the Master will take care of the great lighthouse; *let us keep the lower lights burning.*" Later, the story became a poem set to music, both written by Philip P. Bliss, the song evangelist who worked with Moody and also with Moody's friend, Major D. W. Whittle. This was the favorite hymn of the early-twentieth-century evangelist, Billy Sunday.
[Read or sing stanzas 1 and 2.]

Many people seem to believe that their lives and their witness do not count for much in God's kingdom. But every one of us contacts certain people every day — our neighbors, a friend in the shop or the office, the paper boy or the garbage collector — and for those particular persons, we may provide the only opportunity to hear a personal witness of the gospel. Unless we tell them, they will not hear!

Father Keller of the Christopher Society was once presiding at a large rally in the Coliseum at Los Angeles, California. Suddenly, at a prearranged signal, a switch was pulled and the entire stadium was plunged into darkness. Then Father Keller struck a small match and encouraged each of the 100,000 people present to do the same. In a moment the light from those tiny, flickering matches illuminated the entire amphitheatre. Our light of Christian witness may be small, but it does count, especially when it is added to that of other believers.

In explaining the imagery found in this gospel song, we might say that the great beam of the lighthouse represents the Bible, a Christian magazine, a gospel broadcast, or some outstanding preacher in a historic church pulpit. But each of us is a "lower light" whose gleam is needed to point lost souls to the safety of the harbor, Jesus Christ.

The last stanza of this hymn may not be immediately understood by today's younger generation. It refers to the kerosene lamps and lanterns which were common in Bliss's day and which were still being used in our house and barn when I was a boy on the farm. I remember that it was important that the wick be trimmed regularly – that all the charred part be removed – so that the lamp would burn brightly and evenly and not smoke up the protecting glass.

Each of us has only one light to give to the world. So it is important that we keep it burning brightly, and that all the charrings of sin and selfishness be taken away. This is the same spiritual experience that Jesus talked about in John 15:2: "Every branch that beareth fruit, he purgeth it, that it may bring forth more fruit." Trimming the wick – like pruning a vine – may be painful, especially to our pride, but it results in a brighter witness and a more fruitful life.

The light of the life of Philip Bliss – author of this hymn – burned brightly, but only for a few years. At the age of thirty-eight, while traveling to Chicago for an engagement at the Moody Tabernacle, both he and his wife were killed in a train accident. Yet, through the many hymns he wrote, his lamp of Christian influence still shines and lights the way to faith in God.

"Let your light so shine before men, that they may see your good works, and glorify your Father which is in heaven" (Matt. 5:16).

[Read or sing the last stanza.]

Be thou my vision

[*Crusader Hymns*, No. 147]

The hymn "Be Thou My Vision" is a prayer that we may accept Christ as our pattern, our hero, our ideal. Our adoration is told in these names and phrases: "Lord of my heart," "my best thought," "my Wisdom," "my true Word," "my great Father," "mine inheritance," "my Treasure," and finally "Heart of my own heart."

The original version of this hymn was written by an unknown Irish Christian in the eighth century. The tune is an Irish folk melody. Only in the last few years have both the words and the music become widely known and loved, especially among young people.
[Read or sing stanza 1.]

One of the phrases that is quoted most frequently in political rallies, in sales promotion meetings, and even in the pulpit, is taken from the wise sayings of Solomon: "Where there is no vision, the people perish" (Prov. 29:18).

Idealism is one of the normal, yet remarkable qualities of human personality. Most men and women dream of better things than they now experience. For some, the goal is a better job with more pay, so they might be able to buy what we call the "good things" of life. Others plan for a better education, in order that life might be enriched through service in one of the professions. A scientist envisions a world that is free of killing disease, and so devotes his life to research. An artist dreams of new expressions of beauty, and goes on to create them. Without an ideal, a dream, a vision, a man will not have the incentive to work and to discipline himself in order to achieve these better things. An anonymous author has written:

A vision without a task is a dream;
A task without a vision is drudgery;
A vision and a task is the hope of the world.

Most of us know *individuals* whom we idolize — those whom we consciously or unconsciously revere and would like to imitate. This may be the cheap type of hero worship which surrounds our entertainment "stars;" actually, we are simply impressed because we think they are "famous" or "talented" or "rich." If we really *knew* them, we might discover that, despite their apparent success, they are quite unhappy people who are basically unsuccessful in achieving personal peace and poise. They would then rather quickly cease to be our "heroes." As Ralph Waldo Emerson said, "Every hero becomes a bore at last."

However, there is a valid and valuable type of hero-worship. Those of us who have loving and wise parents hold them up as ideals, even though as teenagers we may have seemed to be "sparring" with them. We give this sort of recognition to the teachers and coaches who have participated in our educational and physical growth. When we read the biographies of great men of other eras, or share their artistic and philosophical achievements, we often admire and seek to emulate them as well.

If our heroes are really worthy persons of great accomplishment and high ideals, hero worship is a good thing because *we become like the things or the people we idolize.* But, as someone has said, "No man is a hero to his valet." Whether we are thinking of parents, of teachers and pastors, or of the great men of the present or past, sooner or later we find something in their lives which spoils the "hero image," something we would not want to copy.

There is one hero whom it is safe to worship and to imitate in every aspect of personality and behavior; He is Jesus Christ. Men of every generation have echoed the judgment of Pilate, the Roman governor who sent Him to death – "I find no fault in him." Every outward action of Jesus' life reflected only perfect love, personal peace and mature, balanced personality. And, if we were able to read His mind, we would discover that every thought and motive was also perfect. Not only was He free from all evil; He also possessed every good thing.

We have recently heard a lot of discussion about whether or not the "Beatles" are more popular than Jesus, as one of their members insisted. Long after the "Beatles" are only vaguely remembered as one of the youthful entertainment groups in the 1960's, young men and women will still declare their allegiance to Christ. He is a worthy and a lasting hero!

[Read or sing stanzas 2-4.]

Be Thou my Vision, O Lord of my heart;
Nought be all else to me, save that Thou art –
Thou my best thought, by day or by night,
Waking or sleeping, Thy presence my light.

Be Thou my Wisdom, and Thou my true Word;
I ever with Thee and Thou with me, Lord;
Thou my great Father, I Thy true son;
Thou in me dwelling, and I with Thee one.

Riches I heed not, nor man's empty praise,
Thou mine inheritance, now and always:
Thou and Thou only, first in my heart,
High King of heaven, my Treasure Thou art.

High King of heaven, my victory won,
May I reach heaven's joys, O bright heaven's Sun!
Heart of my own heart, whatever befall,
Still be my Vision, O Ruler of all.

Ancient Irish
Trans. by Mary E. Byrne (1880-1931)
Versified by Eleanor H. Hull (1860-1935)

Have Thine own way, Lord! have Thine own way!
Thou art the Potter; I am the clay.
Mold me and make me after Thy will,
While I am waiting, yielded and still.

Have Thine own way, Lord! have Thine own way!
Search me and try me, Master, today!
Whiter than snow, Lord, wash me just now,
As in Thy presence humbly I bow.

Have Thine own way, Lord! have Thine own way!
Wounded and weary, help me, I pray!
Power — all power — surely is Thine!
Touch me and heal me, Saviour divine!

Have Thine own way, Lord! have Thine own way!
Hold o'er my being absolute sway!
Fill with Thy Spirit till all shall see
Christ only, always, living in me!

Adelaide A. Pollard (1862-1934)

Have Thine Own Way, Lord

[*Crusader Hymns,* No. 154]

As she sat in a prayer meeting service early in this century, Adelaide Pollard was so depressed that she could hardly concentrate on what was being said. She had felt a heavy burden on her heart for the continent of Africa and was convinced that God wanted her to go as a missionary. She had been on the verge of preparing to sail, but now it was evident that the necessary funds could not be raised and her plans had to be canceled. Into her dark mood a few words filtered; it was part of the prayer of an old lady she knew: "It's all right, Lord! It doesn't matter what you bring into our lives; just have your own way with us!" Suddenly she found that her burden had lifted; in her own submission to the will of God she had found peace.

After returning home that evening, Miss Pollard meditated on the story of the potter, found in Jeremiah 18:3,4:

> **Then I went down to the potter's house, and, behold, he wrought a work on the wheels.**
>
> **And the vessel that he made of clay was marred in the hand of the potter: so he made it again another vessel, as seemed good to the potter to make it.**

The words seemed to describe the experiences of her own life. Born in Iowa in 1862, she had been well trained and for several years had taught in a girls' school. She was also a talented writer of both prose and poetry and produced many religious articles and some hymns. But her real interest was in evangelism, and soon she began a ministry of Bible teaching. Traveling widely throughout the United States, she spoke to numerous groups and churches.

Throughout her early life, Adelaide Pollard had a consuming interest in foreign missions. For a time, she taught at the Missionary Training Institute at Nyack, New York, hoping that she might herself serve as a missionary. And now it seemed that God, who had been molding her life all along, had suddenly deserted her. "But," she thought, "perhaps my questioning of God's will shows a flaw in my life, so God has decided to break me, as the potter broke the defective vessel, and then to mold my life again *in His own pattern.*"

The words of a poem took shape in her mind, even as her heart bowed in a new consecration — "Thou art the Potter, I am the clay. Mold me and make me after Thy will, While I am waiting, yielded and still."
[Read or sing stanza 1.]

As she continued to write, Miss Pollard acknowledged that the assertion of man's own will is the basic sin he commits before God. As unsaved men and women, we go our own way living as we please, assuming that God has no claim on us. And, even after we know Christ as Saviour, the sin which creeps into our lives is also centered in the ego — self-consciousness, self-centeredness, and self-will.

Sometimes we even sin while doing God's work, when we insist on doing it in our own way and according to our own time schedule. Perhaps this had happened in the planning of her trip to Africa, and in the frustration that arose when her plans fell through. And so, in contrition, she wrote again, "Search me and try me, Master, today! Whiter than snow, Lord, wash me just now, As in Thy presence humbly I bow."
[Read or sing stanzas 2 and 3.]

The life of selflessness which God desires is expressed in Paul's words, "I have been crucified with Christ: and I myself no longer live, but Christ lives in me" (Gal. 2:20, *Living Letters*). These words are the basis of the hymn's final stanza.
[Read or sing stanza 4.]

In God's own time He allowed Adelaide Pollard to minister in Africa. She also spent several years in England during the first World War, and then returned to her traveling ministry in America. She continued to speak publicly until she was 72 years of age when, on her way to yet another engagement, she was taken ill in a railroad station in New York City. Soon after, she died.

So ended the remarkable life of a frail, little woman who was so modest that her hymns were signed only by her initials. She had learned that God uses the person who will sincerely pray, "Have Thine Own Way, Lord."

TO GOD BE THE GLORY

[*Crusader Hymns,* No. 3]

A Hymn Story by Cliff Barrows

If a hymn die, can it live again? The life-story of "To God Be the Glory" proves that the answer is "yes!" Originally composed in America sometime before 1875, it was almost immediately forgotten in its native land. In 1954, however, "To God Be the Glory" was rediscovered and acclaimed as a new favorite.

In Great Britain this same hymn never faded into oblivion as it did in the United States. I had heard it sung there in 1952 during one of our early visits. Later, it was suggested for inclusion in the songbook we were compiling for the London crusade of 1954. Because of its strong text of praise and its attractive melody, I agreed. We introduced the hymn during the early days of those meetings in Harringay Arena. As a result, Billy Graham asked that we repeat it often because he was impressed with the enthusiastic participation of the audience. In the closing weeks of the crusade it became our theme hymn, repeated almost every night. The words well expressed our praise to God, who was doing wondrous things in Britain.

Returning to America, we brought the hymn with us and used it first in the Nashville, Tennessee crusade of August, 1954. It was quickly adopted by many church groups and has recently been included in several new hymnals, including the *Baptist Hymnal* (Southern Baptist) and *Trinity Hymnal* (Orthodox Presbyterian).

Why "To God Be the Glory" was so late in achieving recognition in its homeland may always remain a mystery. It is not mentioned in the writings of either Fanny Crosby, author of the words, or W. H. Doane, composer of the music. Evidently the songleader Ira D. Sankey took it to Great Britain when he went there with evangelist D. L. Moody in 1873. Sankey included it in his *Sacred Songs and Solos,* a hymnbook first published in England in 1874 and still used today.

For some unknown reason, the song did not appear in the important *Gospel Hymns* series of books which Sankey published in America after his return from Britain in 1875. Through the years, "To God Be the Glory" *has* been included in several American hymnals. But until 1954, it failed to find its rightful place in the singing of our congregations.

Of all the songs that have been popularized through crusade activity, we are most happy about this one. Its testimony should rebound in the heart of every Christian; every area of a person's life should reflect this witness, "To God Be the Glory."

All men — Christian or non-Christian — try to find meaning in life. Modern existentialists, atheists and agnostics (and even a few who call themselves Christians) are trying to find this meaning *within man himself.* But the true answer to this quest is defined in the *Westminster Catechism:* "The chief end of man is to glorify God, and to enjoy Him forever." In other words, the reason for man's creation and the whole purpose of his living is to express praise of God, with his lips and with his life.

We give God glory because of His love, a love which provided redemption for mankind. The Apostle Paul exclaimed, "God forbid that I should glory, save in the cross of our Lord Jesus Christ" (Gal. 6:14). We bring nothing to our own salvation; it is all of God. Therefore we can take no credit for it. To God be the glory!

In another passage, Paul reminds us: "For ye are bought with a price: therefore glorify God in your body, and in your spirit, which are God's" (I Cor. 6:20). This is the Biblical answer to the seeking existentialist. Each day's experiences have ultimate meaning only if we acknowledge that we are God's, and that each act and each thought should glorify Him. To God be the glory!

Billy Graham often reminds us team members that this is especially true in the full-time Christian vocations. God has chosen to use *men* to spread His "good news," the gospel. Because we live in a Madison Avenue world of culture and communication, the names of preachers and evangelists are sometimes advertised widely. But we will be in serious trouble if we imagine that the crusade ministry is possible because of us or our talents. It is all of God, who has declared "My glory will I not give to another" (Isaiah 42:8). To God be the glory!

A challenge for each day of each Christian's life is found in Matthew 5:16: "Let your light so shine before men, that they may see your good works and glorify your Father which is in heaven." We should be thankful if others feel that we have been gracious and loving in our relations with them. But we dare not keep the praise for ourselves! It is God who enables us to be Christ-like. To God be the glory!

[Read or sing the entire hymn.]

To God be the glory, great things He hath done,
So loved He the world that He gave us His Son,
Who yielded His life an atonement for sin,
And opened the Lifegate that all may go in.

O perfect redemption, the purchase of blood,
To every believer the promise of God;
The vilest offender who truly believes,
That moment from Jesus a pardon receives.

Great things He hath taught us, great things He hath done,
And great our rejoicing thro' Jesus the Son;
But purer, and higher, and greater will be
Our wonder, our transport, when Jesus we see.

Refrain:

Praise the Lord, praise the Lord,
Let the earth hear His voice!
Praise the Lord, praise the Lord,
Let the people rejoice!
O come to the Father thro' Jesus the Son,
And give Him the glory, great things He hath done.

Fanny J. Crosby (1820-1915)

For all the saints who from their labors rest,
Who Thee by faith before the world confessed,
Thy name, O Jesus, be forever blest.
Alleluia!

Thou wast their rock, their fortress and their might;
Thou, Lord, their captain in the well-fought fight;
Thou, in the darkness drear, their one true light.
Alleluia!

O blest communion, fellowship divine!
We feebly struggle; they in glory shine.
Yet all are one in Thee, for all are Thine.
Alleluia!

And when the strife is fierce, the warfare long,
Steals on the ear the distant triumph song,
And hearts are brave again and arms are strong.
Alleluia!

The golden evening brightens in the west;
Soon, soon to faithful warriors cometh rest;
And sweet the calm of Paradise, the blest.
Alleluia!

But lo! there breaks a yet more glorious day;
The saints triumphant rise in bright array;
The King of Glory passes on His way.
Alleluia!

From earth's wide bounds, from ocean's farthest coast,
Thro' gates of pearl stream in the countless host,
Singing to Father, Son, and Holy Ghost.
Alleluia!

William W. How (1823-1897)

For All the Saints

[*Crusader Hymns*, No. 245]

A Hymn Story by Don Hustad

[Read or sing stanzas 1 and 2.]

Often in life, in order to avoid an error of one kind, we move so far in the other direction that we make an equally regrettable mistake. This principle may apply to our conception of sainthood. We are certainly right when we refuse to exalt departed Christians to such a degree that we would pray to them. However, we are wrong when we relegate God's men of the past to antiquity. We can learn much from them and should be thankful anew for the contributions that they have made. In our "forward-looking" twentieth century, we may be especially guilty of this error of neglect.

What then is the truth behind the phrase in the Apostles' creed, "I believe in the communion of saints"? Samuel J. Stone's hymn, "The Church's One Foundation," says that Christians today possess "mystic sweet communion with those whose rest is won." In the third stanza of Bishop How's memorial hymn "For All the Saints," it is expressed in these phrases: "O blest communion, fellowship divine! We feebly struggle; they in glory shine. Yet all are one in Thee, for all are Thine."

Some people insist that the citizens of heaven can observe what goes on in the world. But, can we be sure that bygone saints are sharing our specific problems and victories? As the hymn says, those in heaven are now resting from their labors. For them the struggle of life is over, and they now sing the song of triumph. Though we are all part of the Church – the body of Christ – ours is a mystic, a mysterious communion. Those who have died are the "church triumphant;" those of us who still live make up the "church militant."

The occupants of heaven must know that God is still working in the world through people like us, to further His kingdom. Certainly we can be encouraged by the examples and the wisdom they have left us from their earthly pilgrimage. This is the fellowship – the sharing – the communion of the saints – that the hymn is talking about.

The eleventh chapter of Hebrews has been called the "Westminster Abbey" of the scriptures. As many of the honored British dead are memorialized in that ancient church, so God's heroes are remembered in this chapter. When we review the lives of both Old Testament and New Testament saints, we are reminded over and over that God is faithful and all-powerful. He will be the final victor in the battle against evil.

There is another truth we should remember. Because God is faithful, Spirit-filled *men* can *also* be faithful and victorious, doing great things for God in spite of the temptations and persecutions which might beset them. As the writer infers in Hebrews 12:1, these saints are all witnesses to the power of the gospel. Because of their witness, we take fresh courage for the battle. Through their example, we are challenged to "lay aside every weight, and the sin which doth so easily beset us, and . . . run with patience the race that is set before us."

[Read or sing stanzas 3-5.]

Each of us will have a different group of "saints" to whom we give honor because of the contributions they have made to our lives. In addition to many of the Bible personalities, I have personally been challenged by the musicians and the hymnists who have given so much to the church. I owe a debt of gratitude to John of Damascus, Ambrose of Milan, Bernard of Clairvaux, Luther, Calvin, Sweelinck, Johann Walther, the Bach family, the Wesleys, Lowell Mason and many more.

The author of this hymn deserves to be noted for his contributions to God's work. William Walsham How, born into a wealthy Anglican family in 1823 and educated at Oxford, gave his entire life in sacrificial service to God. He was known as the "omnibus bishop" because he scorned the private coach he could afford, and rode public transportation alongside his poor parishioners in London's East End. How wrote about sixty hymns, of which twenty-five are still in use. Among them are the favorites "We Give Thee but Thine Own," "O Word of God Incarnate," and "O Jesus, Thou Art Standing."

In your prayers today, remember and thank God for the people, both living and dead, to whom you owe so much. In addition to my family heritage, I am grateful for the memory of preachers and Bible expositors who introduced me to Jesus Christ. Also influential in my life were others: a modest little piano teacher who encouraged me to begin practicing when I was four, a Primitive Methodist pastor who helped me go to college, and many music instructors who opened my mind and heart to the wonders of sound.

For whom do you give thanks to God?

[Read or sing stanzas 6 and 7.]

Wherever He Leads I'll Go

[*Crusader Hymns*, No. 215]

A Hymn Story by Billy Graham

In January of 1936, the Southern Baptist songwriter B. B. McKinney was leading the music at the Alabama Sunday School Convention which was held that year in the town of Clanton. The featured speaker was the Reverend R. S. Jones, McKinney's friend of many years, who because of ill health had recently returned from missionary service in Brazil.

The two men were visiting over dinner one evening when Mr. Jones revealed to Dr. McKinney that his physicians would not allow him to return to South America. When asked about his future plans the missionary said, "I don't know, but wherever He leads I'll go." The words stuck in Dr. McKinney's mind, and before the convention's evening session began, he had written both the words and music of this song. At the close of Mr. Jones' message, Dr. McKinney related this story and sang "Wherever He Leads I'll Go" to the congregation. [Read or sing stanza 1.]

The opening words of the song, "Take up thy cross and follow me," contain one of Jesus' most penetrating challenges to his disciples – a statement so significant that it is found in each of the four gospels. Luke 9:23 states: "If any man will come after me, let him deny himself, and take up his cross daily, and follow me." In *The New English Bible* the same verse begins, "If anyone wishes to be a follower of mine, he must leave self behind." *Living Gospels* gives this paraphrase: "Anyone who wants to follow me must put aside his own desires and conveniences."

The original Greek New Testament has an even stronger inference than any of these. There the words used for "deny himself" can be translated "I don't even know that man!" This kind of selflessness is hard for most people to understand. Even when Christians understand it, performance is hard to achieve! Just how does this attitude manifest itself in everyday life?

A member of your church may be asked to teach a Sunday school class. Because of inborn timidity, his natural response is to refuse and even to believe that the refusal is a sign of humility. But, in the same situation, the dedicated Christian will accept the opportunity to serve, saying of himself, "Who is that shy and fearful 'self'? I don't know any such person!" This is "denying one's self" and it is a healthy attitude, psychologically and spiritually!

And what does it mean to "take up your cross?" Does this phrase suggest that the Christian should expect to carry heavy burdens? I believe it implies much more than that. The cross was an instrument of public execution. If Christ were speaking today, He would say, "Take up your gallows (or your electric chair) and follow me." The Apostle Paul explained this command when he said, "I have been crucified with Christ: and I myself no longer live, but Christ lives in me" (Gal. 2:20, *Living Letters*). It is our inner self-centeredness which dies when we yield to a higher will than our own. God's will replaces ours, and then Christ truly lives within us.

Living on this higher plane provides a new response to the situations of life. When a cruel and false accusation is made against us, our natural reaction is to fight back, to vindicate ourselves. If the story wasn't true, we feel justified in returning the insult. But to the person living on a Christ-centered level, the "self" who was criticized is dead – crucified. How can a dead "self" talk back?

The reality of the indwelling Christ is demonstrated by selflessness in all the important decisions of life. Such a dedication is what the hymn "Wherever He Leads I'll Go" is mostly all about. Of course, we may have a personal interest in one vocation or another or a preference to live in this location or that. But when we "follow Christ" we must ask ourselves, "What decision does He want me to make? Where does Christ want me to serve? And how?"

For some, it will be a glorious privilege to serve God as a pastor, a missionary, an evangelist, a teacher, or a church musician. This hymn is certainly a good one to sing when a challenge for missionary service is given. But don't forget that its inspiration came from a missionary who could not return to the field! Reverend Jones spent the rest of his life serving with the Southern Baptist Relief and Annuity Board.

Other Christians too will have the no-less-glorious honor of serving Christ as a homemaker, a doctor, a draftsman, or a farmer. In every instance, our life's work should be determined by God's call, not just our whims and desires. When this is true, even washing dishes becomes a sacrament, as proclaimed in the motto my wife has posted in her kitchen: "Divine services conducted here three times daily."
[Read or sing stanzas 2-4.]

"Take up thy cross and follow me,"
I heard my Master say;
"I gave my life to ransom thee,
Surrender your all today."

He drew me closer to His side,
I sought His will to know,
And in that will I now abide,
Wherever He leads I'll go.

It may be through the shadows dim,
Or o'er the stormy sea,
I take my cross and follow Him,
Wherever He leadeth me.

My heart, my life, my all I bring
To Christ who loves me so;
He is my Master, Lord, and King,
Wherever He leads I'll go.

Refrain:

Wherever He leads I'll go,
Wherever He leads I'll go,
I'll follow my Christ who loves me so,
Wherever He leads I'll go.

B. B. McKinney (1886-1952)

Holy God, we praise Thy name;
Lord of all, we bow before Thee;
All on earth Thy scepter claim,
All in heav'n above adore Thee.
Infinite Thy vast domain,
Everlasting is Thy reign.

Hark, the loud celestial hymn
Angel choirs above are raising;
Cherubim and seraphim,
In unceasing chorus praising,
Fill the heav'ns with sweet accord:
Holy, holy, holy Lord.

Lo! the apostolic train
Joins Thy sacred name to hallow;
Prophets swell the glad refrain,
And the white-robed martyrs follow;
And, from morn to set of sun,
Through the Church the song goes on.

Holy Father, Holy Son,
Holy Spirit, Three we name Thee;
While in essence only One,
Undivided God we claim Thee,
And adoring bend the knee,
While we sing our praise to Thee.

From the *Te Deum*, 4th Century
German poem, 18th Century
Trans. by Clarence Walworth (1820-1900)

Holy God, We Praise Thy Name

[*Crusader Hymns*, No. 11]

One hymn that will always be used, whenever a crusade is conducted on the continent of Europe, is "Holy God, We Praise Thy Name." In Germany – and this is where, in the eighteenth century, the hymn as we know it first appeared – it begins "Grosser Gott, wir loben Dich." In France, it is "Grand Dieu, nous te benissons" and in Denmark, "Almagt Gud, velsignet vaer."

The original text is much older and is a part of the fourth century *Te Deum*. This ancient canticle has been called the "greatest of all non-scriptural hymns in Latin," and is sung around the world in some form and some language by most Christians. In the Anglican communion, for instance, it is used each Sunday in the service of Morning Prayer.

Through the years there has been a great deal of conjecture as to the authorship of this historic poem. One old legend maintained that it was improvised responsively by St. Ambrose and St. Augustine, when the latter was baptized. Others have credited it to Hilary of Gaul (the first known Latin hymnist) or to Charlemagne the Great. Scholars today believe that it is probably the work of a missionary-bishop, Niceta, whose field was Remesiana in Dacia, which is now part of Jugoslavia. In his writings, St. Jerome gives Niceta credit for spreading the gospel among the fourth century European barbarians, and refers to his method as by "sweet songs of the cross."

The entire *Te Deum* is a very long hymn of praise in three parts. The stanza-version, "Holy God, We Praise Thy Name," is taken from the first phrases, which appear this way in English prose:

We praise thee, O God; we acknowledge thee to be the Lord. All the earth doth worship thee, the Father everlasting. To thee all angels cry aloud; the heavens and all the powers therein; To thee cherubim and seraphim continually do cry, "Holy, holy, holy, Lord God of Sabaoth; heaven and earth are full of the majesty of thy glory."

The glorious company of the apostles praise thee. The goodly fellowship of the prophets praise thee. The noble army of martyrs praise thee. The holy church throughout all the world doth acknowledge thee; the Father of an infinite majesty; thine adorable, true and only Son; also the Holy Ghost, the Comforter.

The enduring quality and extensive use of this hymn must be representative of mankind's deepest need — to express a relationship with God. Otherwise, why should Christians speak or sing their worship of God at all? The response to this question as posed in a typical Sunday school class or in family devotions would be, "We praise God because of what He has done for us." Such a response to God's providence is certainly a good reason for worship, but is it the highest incentive?

The word "worship" is of Anglo-Saxon origin. It was once spelled "woerth-scipe" and meant "to ascribe worth." Here then is the purest and most basic motive for worship: of all the beings and objects in the universe, God alone is *worthy* of our praise. He is worthy, first of all, because of *what He is* — perfectly holy, all-knowing, all-powerful, never-changing and everywhere present.

It is not a sign of irreverence or unbelief to say that God is also inscrutable; we can never know or understand Him completely. He has said, "As the heavens are higher than the earth, so are my ways higher than your ways, and my thoughts than your thoughts" (Isaiah 55:9).

What God has done stems from *what He is;* to praise Him for His works as well as His character is certainly proper. He is the Creator, Sustainer and Redeemer of the universe. He is our Heavenly Father, and is concerned about our great need of salvation and our smaller needs of comfort, guidance, protection and material necessities.

The angels in heaven have never experienced God's love as we do, yet they worship Him continually. How much more praise we have to render to God in proportion, yet how inadequate our response may be! As you read or sing the stanzas of this hymn, and as you carry on your activities today, remember the attributes of the God who dwells about you and within you. Praise Him for what He has done for others and for you. Praise Him also just because He is worthy to be praised!

[Read or sing the entire hymn.]

WE LIFT OUR VOICE REJOICING

[*Crusader Hymns*, No. 14]

A Hymn Story by Cliff Barrows

[Read or sing stanza 1.]

"O sing unto the Lord a new song" is a challenge often repeated in the scriptures. This means that we should not be satisfied with yesterday's Christian experiences. Each new day should bring a better understanding of God and a growing relationship with Christ. And our daily spiritual victories should be expressed in fresh words of testimony and prayer, and also in new songs of faith and worship.

To encourage the writing and singing of new hymns, in 1961 the Billy Graham Evangelistic Association conducted a "new hymn contest" together with the National Church Music Fellowship. The winning title chosen from over 900 entries was "We Lift Our Voice Rejoicing" written by the Reverend Jack W. Hayford, a youth leader and later dean of students at L.I.F.E. Bible College in Los Angeles, California. The following is Mr. Hayford's own story of how his song was written:

> **We had just concluded a conference held in the splendor of the autumn-spangled hills near Estes Park, Colorado, in 1960. The grand old hymn "To God Be the Glory" had themed the series there, and returning to Los Angeles I would hum that melody and nostalgically meditate on the beauty and blessing found during those days in the Rockies. Yet as excellent as that praiseful song is, something within me yearned to give vent to a *personal* expression of worship.**
>
> **One evening, as I left the office for home, the song came to me. Completely without labored premeditation, sparked by a glimpse of the clear, wind-driven sky which served as a backdrop to a single tree being stripped of its leaves, the words poured forth, together with the melody of the first two lines: "We lift our voice, rejoicing, because the Lord above hath sent His Son to save us and manifest His love." I turned the corner, and was confronted by the mountains north of the city. Walking briskly I added the next words: "Let every hill re-echo to this the song we raise;" then the words of the ransomed multitude in Revelation, chapter five, came to mind — "To Him whose blood hath brought us be glory, power and praise."**
>
> **It was as though the autumn atmosphere had served as a catalyst to unleash the joy of the Lord in my soul. God's own natural creation provided the setting, and His new creative work in me produced the song. Arriving home I went immediately to my study, and within minutes the hymn was completed. The overflow of my heart was on the paper before me.**

A rich satisfaction came as I completed the song. It was the fulfillment sensed when you are able to express the emotion of a given moment; in this case, a moment when my heart thrilled at the wonder of God's creative power and the grandeur of His saving grace. For my part, at least, the hymn became a means by which I could sing to myself the praise of the living God.

Many Christians share in similar moments of spiritual exaltation when their whole being is in harmony with God the Creator. Few there are, however, that are able to capture the sensitivity of such an experience in song or the written word. Perhaps the expression of our own hymn of praise in a uniquely personal manner is limited to private devotions.

On the other hand, some Christians may develop their techniques in the use of language and melody to the point where God can use them extensively. Such a person is the author of this hymn, Jack Hayford. He recalls the time when he heard the late Phil Kerr tell the stories of famous hymns and their writers. Then fourteen years old, Hayford thought: "How wonderful! Though these men and women have long since died, their ministry still continues. How I would love to write something that would outlive me, that would be sung throughout the world by the people of God." Mr. Hayford's desire has been granted through the several fine songs that he has written.

Whether we write a hymn or simply join God's people in singing it, our lives and our lips should bring a new "offering of praise" to our Lord each day.

[Read or sing stanzas 2 and 3.]

We lift our voice rejoicing,
Because the Lord above
Hath sent His Son to save us,
And manifest His love.
Let every hill re-echo
With this the song we raise,
"To Him whose blood hath bought us
Be glory, pow'r and praise."

We lift our eyes in faith to
The cross whereon He died,
Redeemed at matchless price, now
In Christ we're justified.
His blood hath washed our garments,
His peace hath filled our souls,
The cross is now our glory
Since grace hath made us whole.

We lift our hearts to worship
The conquering Saviour's name,
Our tongues speak forth the praises
Of Him who is the same.
Christ Jesus reigns in power
Throughout eternity.
As yesterday, so now, and
Forever He shall be.

Refrain:

We praise Thee, O Father,
Unspeakable our joy,
In Christ our hearts find glory
Sin's pow'r can not destroy.

Jack W. Hayford (b. 1934)

Come, Thou Almighty King,
Help us Thy name to sing,
Help us to praise:
Father, all glorious,
O'er all victorious,
Come, and reign over us,
Ancient of Days.

Come, Thou Incarnate Word,
Gird on Thy mighty sword,
Our prayer attend:
Come, and Thy people bless,
And give Thy word success:
Spirit of holiness,.
On us descend.

Come, Holy Comforter,
Thy sacred witness bear
In this glad hour:
Thou who almighty art,
Now rule in every heart,
And ne'er from us depart,
Spirit of power.

To the great One in Three
Eternal praises be
Hence, evermore!
His sovereign majesty
May we in glory see,
And to eternity
Love and adore!

Source Unknown

Come, Thou Almighty King

[*Crusader Hymns*, No. 28]

"Come, Thou Almighty King" is a hymn for which we have little or no background. Although it is one of the best known English hymns, we do not even know who wrote it. The text first appeared in a little pamphlet in 1757, together with a hymn by Charles Wesley. It too may be a Wesley hymn, but no hymnologist has ever claimed that it is.

The rhythm and meter of this hymn are most unusual; in fact, only one other hymn — "God save our gracious king," the British national anthem — uses it, and *that* melody was first used for *these* words. "God Save the King" had appeared about fifteen years earlier, and it seems as if "Come, Thou Almighty King" may have been conceived as a sequel to it. One hymn is a prayer for an earthly ruler; the other is a prayer to a heavenly King.

Some churchgoers who sing these words frequently may not have noticed that this is a Trinity hymn. Each of the first three stanzas is addressed to a different member of the God-head, and the last stanza to "the great One in Three." The first verse speaks to God the Father, our Almighty King, and is a prayer that He will help us to sing His praise. The last phrase mentions a name of God which is given in Daniel 7:22. "Ancient of Days" speaks of God's eternity, his timelessness. He has always existed and He will always exist.

[Read or sing stanza 1.]

The second stanza, addressed to God the Son, reminds us of the opening words of John's gospel: "In the beginning was the Word, and the Word was with God, and the Word was God." Here is a prayer to Jesus Christ who is God incarnate, God in the flesh. In Revelation 19, John's vision of Christ, we read that "his name is called The Word of God" (verse 13) and that "out of his mouth goeth a sharp sword, that with it he should smite the nations" (verse 15). Yes, Christ came the first time to be our Redeemer; He will come again to be our Judge.

[Read or sing stanza 2.]

If any songleader is tempted to omit the third stanza when singing this hymn, we would remind him not to slight the third person of the Trinity. For this is a prayer to God the Holy Spirit, the "Holy Comforter." The name here actually means "Paraclete" (Advocate or

Lawyer) because the Holy Spirit represents Jesus Christ, now that the Son has returned to His Father in heaven. One of these lines reminds us that it is the Holy Spirit who "beareth witness with our Spirit, that we are the children of God." Another phrase declares that, although God's Spirit is almighty, He can only rule our hearts when we allow Him to do so.

[Read or sing stanza 3.]

The truth of the Trinity, that God is One yet Three or "One in Three," cannot fully be understood. Many scholars have tried to probe its mystery and to express it in words. One of them, a certain Joseph Dare, has said: "Steam is water, and ice is water, and water is water; these three are one."

John Wesley once said: "Tell me how it is that in this room there are three candles and but one light, and I will explain to you the mode of the divine existence."

The late A. W. Tozer has written:

> **Some persons who reject all they cannot explain have denied that God is a Trinity. Subjecting the Most High to their cold, level-eyed scrutiny, they conclude that it is impossible that He could be both One and Three. These forget that their whole life is enshrouded in mystery. They fail to consider that any real explanation of even the simplest phenomenon in nature lies hidden in obscurity and can no more be explained than can the mystery of the Godhead . . .**
>
> **The doctrine of the Trinity . . . is truth for the heart. The fact that it cannot be satisfactorily explained, instead of being against it, is in its favor. Such a truth had to be revealed; no one could have imagined it. (*The Knowledge of The Holy,* Harper and Row, 1961; pp. 25, 31. Used by permission.)**

[Read or sing stanza 4.]

Trust and Obey

[*Crusader Hymns*, No. 181]

A Hymn Story by Cliff Barrows

I first learned to know the great songs of the church as a boy in Sunday school in Ceres, California. Sometime later I was drafted to be the third member of a family trio, singing with my two younger sisters. It seemed to me then that we were too often called upon to perform—at church services, youth rallies and camps, and even at weddings and funerals!

Consequently, as a growing boy, I must admit that hymn-singing was occasionally more pain than pleasure. But in later life, the hymnbook became one of my most important resources for personal worship. Today, I am thankful that I was required to memorize so many hymns at an early age. They will probably never leave my subconscious.

One of my longtime favorites, which is always included in crusade songbooks, is "Trust and Obey." The music for this song was composed by D. B. Towner, the first director of music at Moody Bible Institute in Chicago. The inspiration for the hymn's writing came in 1886 during an occasion when Towner was leading singing for D. L. Moody in Brockton, Massachusetts. In a testimony service which took place, he heard a young man say, "I am not quite sure—but I am going to trust, and I am going to obey."

Towner jotted down the words and sent them to his friend J. H. Sammis, a Presbyterian minister, who developed the idea into a full hymn. The refrain came first—it is a capsule version of the entire song—and the verses later.
[Read or sing stanzas 1 and 2.]

The song emphasizes the two aspects of being a Christian—faith and good works. And it places them in proper order! We come to Christ without any plea "but that He has shed His blood" for us. "For it is by His grace you are saved, through trusting Him; it is not your own doing" (Eph. 2:8, *New English Bible*).

But *after* we trust in Christ, our faith must be translated into action. Because God loves us and we love Him, we seek to obey Him, and to do His will in every realm of our lives. As James asks, "What use is it for a man to say he has faith when he does nothing to show it?" (James 2:14, *NEB*).

I am afraid that some Christians are tempted to think negatively about a commitment of obedience to God. To submit to the commands "to die to self" and "to present your body a living sacrifice" sounds like such a painful thing.

But the truth is clearly stated in this hymn. "We never can prove (experience) the delights of His love, until all on the altar we lay. There's no other way to be happy . . . but to trust and obey." Do we imagine that God who loves us so much would wish us anything less than that which brings us complete fulfillment in life? We can trust God to manage our affairs better than we can ourselves.

D. L. Moody said on one occasion: "The blood (of Christ) alone makes us safe. The Word (of God) alone makes us sure. Obedience (to God) makes us happy." What a formula for a poised and successful life! The death and resurrection of Christ provides a full and free salvation. God's Word assures us that it is settled for all eternity. And allowing God to order our lives each day insures complete serenity and happiness.

Somehow I always associate the message of "Trust and Obey" with Dawson Trotman of the *Navigators*, who worked with us for several years before his untimely death.

"Daws" often brought a message on the TNT of Christian service — "Trust 'n Tackle." The "trust" in this motto implies a complete, childlike confidence in our Heavenly Father, and an obedience to Him in all of life's activities. Then we can be assured of God's strength bolstering us to tackle any challenge that may appear. God will see us through!

[Read or sing stanzas 3 and 4.]

When we walk with the Lord
In the light of His Word,
What a glory He sheds on our way,
While we do His good will
He abides with us still,
And with all who will trust and obey.

Not a shadow can rise,
Not a cloud in the skies,
But His smile quickly drives it away;
Not a doubt nor a fear,
Not a sigh nor a tear,
Can abide while we trust and obey.

But we never can prove
The delights of His love
Until all on the altar we lay;
For the favor He shows,
And the joy He bestows,
Are for them who will trust and obey.

Then in fellowship sweet
We will sit at His feet,
Or we'll walk by His side in the way;
What He says we will do,
Where He sends we will go —
Never fear, only trust and obey.

Refrain:

Trust and obey,
For there's no other way
To be happy in Jesus,
But to trust and obey.

John H. Sammis (1846-1919)

Children of the heavenly Father
Safely in His bosom gather;
Nestling bird nor star in heaven
Such a refuge e'er was given.

God His own doth tend and nourish,
In His holy courts they flourish;
Like a father kind He spares them,
In His loving arms He bears them.

Neither life nor death can ever
From the Lord His children sever;
For His love and deep compassion
Comforts them in tribulation.

What He takes or what He gives us
Shows the Father's love so precious;
We may trust His purpose wholly —
'Tis His children's welfare solely.

Carolina V. (Sandell) Berg (1832-1903)

Children of the Heavenly Father

[*Crusader Hymns*, No. 189]

A Hymn Story by Don Hustad

Throughout the history of the Christian church, most hymnwriters were men: pastors, theologians, monks, bishops and missionaries. But in the nineteenth century, women began to make important contributions to our hymnals. In Great Britain, there were Cecil Frances Alexander and Frances Ridley Havergal; in America, Harriet Beecher Stowe and Fanny J. Crosby; and in Sweden, Lina Sandell, the author of "Children of the Heavenly Father."

Her full name was actually Carolina Vilhelmina Sandell, and she was born in a Lutheran parsonage in 1832. In childhood she was probably known as "daddy's girl." She was not strong physically, and often stayed in her father's study while her classmates were playing outdoors.

Lina's poetic gift showed itself at a very early age. When she was just thirteen her first book of poems was published. This little volume contained some of her best-loved songs. During her lifetime she wrote 650 hymns in all, and 150 of these have been used by the church. "Children of the Heavenly Father" is perhaps the best known. When we took a choir on tour in Scandinavia a few years ago, our singers painstakingly learned the phonetic sounds so we could sing it in Swedish, "Tryggare kan ingen vara."

It does not take long to see that the hymn's basic message is about God's relationship as a Father to us, His children. Many of these phrases are taken almost word-for-word from the Bible. See if you can identify them as you sing the hymn or read the poem.
[Read or sing the entire hymn.]

The Bible tells us: "Not one sparrow (What do they cost? Two for a penny?) can fall to the ground without your Father knowing it" (Matt. 10:29, *Living Gospels*). Scientists tell us that it is impossible to see all the stars in our universe, even with their most powerful telescopes. Yet Psalm 147:4 says that our heavenly Father "telleth the number of the stars: he calleth them all by their names." And God cares more for us than he does for stars and sparrows!

Perhaps the hymn reminded you of these scripture passages as well:

> **He shall feed his flock like a shepherd: he shall gather the lambs with his arm, and carry them in his bosom, and shall gently lead those that are with young (Isa. 40:11).**
>
> **For I am persuaded, that neither death, nor life, nor angels, nor principalities, nor powers, nor things present, nor things to come, nor height, nor depth, nor any other creature, shall be able to separate us from the love of God, which is in Christ Jesus our Lord (Rom. 8:38, 39).**
>
> **The Lord gave and the Lord hath taken away; blessed be the name of the Lord (Job 1:21).**

These stanzas come directly out of the personal experience of Lina Sandell. When she was twenty-six, while taking a boat trip with her father, he fell overboard and she saw him drown. When she lost her earthly father, she learned even more personally the extent of the heavenly Father's love and care.

Recently some theologians have said that we should not think and talk so much of God as a father—that we should grow up and stand on our own two feet, instead of running to God every time we're in a little trouble.

Yet Jesus said in Luke 18:17, "Whosoever shall not receive the kingdom of God as a little child shall in no wise enter therein." And throughout life, as mature men and women, we should remain not childish, but child-like, in our faith and trust, as well as in our obedience to God.

If we do, we can say with confidence: "We know that all that happens to us is working for our good if we love God, and if we are fitting into His plans" (Rom. 8:28, *Living Letters*).

I Surrender All

[*Crusader Hymns*, No. 177]

A Hymn Story by Billy Graham

One of the evangelists who influenced my early preaching was also a hymnist who wrote "I Surrender All"—the Rev. Mr. J. W. Van De Venter. He was a regular visitor at the Florida Bible Institute (now Trinity Bible College) in the late 1930's. We students loved this kind, deeply spiritual gentleman and often gathered in his winter home at Tampa, Florida, for an evening of fellowship and singing.

Mr. Van De Venter was not always a minister. According to his own testimony, his first interest and passion was for art. Having finished college, he taught school for a while in order to finance his continued study of drawing and painting. Later he became supervisor of art in the public schools of Sharon, Pennsylvania.

At that time, evangelistic meetings were being held in his church and Van De Venter became involved in counseling and personal work. Since he had obvious ability in this direction, several of his friends urged him to give up teaching and become an evangelist. For five years he wavered between this challenge and his ambition to become a recognized artist.

As he told the story himself:

> **At last the pivotal hour of my life came and I surrendered all. A new day was ushered into my life. I became an evangelist and discovered down deep in my soul a talent hitherto unknown to me. God had hidden a song in my heart, and touching a tender chord He caused me to sing songs I had never sung before.**

The hymn "I Surrender All" was written some time later in his life, when J. W. Van De Venter recalled this long struggle and final yielding to God's will.

[Read or sing stanzas 1 and 2.]

We begin to surrender to God when we first accept Jesus Christ as Saviour and Lord. The word "Lord" means just that—"Master." At the close of a crusade meeting I ask those who come forward to pray, using these words: "I receive Christ as Saviour; I accept Him as Lord." It is a mistake to think that we can receive Christ's offer of forgiveness and then go out to live our lives as we please. From that moment of commitment, God has a claim on us and we must expect Him to tell us how we should live.

Often this truth comes to an individual in a more forceful way, a little later in his Christian life and walk. A young person may be considering whom he should marry, or what profession he should pursue. A man may be contemplating a new business relationship. A woman may be weighing her obligations to the church, to the community, to her home. Suddenly the true meaning of what the Bible says dawns on them: "Your body is the home of the Holy Spirit God gave you, and . . . He lives within you. Your own body does not belong to you, for God has bought you with a great price. So use every part of your body to give glory back to God, because He owns it" (I Cor. 6:19,20, *Living Letters*).

We should never fear to give God complete control over our lives. He loves us more than we love ourselves, and He will only plan what is best for us. It isn't always true, as it was with Reverend Van De Venter, that God takes us down a different path from that which we would naturally follow. But if He does, we may be sure that it will be a happier and more fruitful life than the one we would have planned for ourselves.

Nor is it true that a person who yields up his own will becomes a weakling—a "mamby-pamby Milquetoast." Just the opposite is true. When we surrender our all to God, we find that we live with a new confidence, a new strength of purpose. No longer do we worry about the decisions we make, for now God is making them; from here on, He is responsible for the outcome. Furthermore, we find that He gives us His own supernatural strength to meet the challenge of each day!

[Read or sing stanzas 3 and 4.]

All to Jesus I surrender,
All to Him I freely give;
I will ever love and trust Him,
In His presence daily live.

All to Jesus I surrender,
Humbly at His feet I bow,
Worldly pleasures all forsaken,
Take me, Jesus, take me now.

All to Jesus I surrender,
Make me, Saviour, wholly Thine;
Let me feel the Holy Spirit,
Truly know that Thou art mine.

All to Jesus I surrender,
Lord, I give myself to Thee;
Fill me with Thy love and power,
Let Thy blessing fall on me.

Refrain:

I surrender all,
I surrender all.
All to Thee, my blessed Saviour,
I surrender all.

Judson W. Van De Venter (1855-1939)

We praise Thee, O God,
For the Son of Thy love,
For Jesus who died
And is now gone above.

We praise Thee, O God,
For Thy Spirit of light,
Who has shown us our Saviour
And scattered our night.

All glory and praise
To the Lamb that was slain,
Who has borne all our sins,
And has cleansed every stain.

Revive us again,
Fill each heart with Thy love;
May each soul be rekindled
With fire from above.

Refrain:

Hallelujah! Thine the glory,
Hallelujah! Amen;
Hallelujah! Thine the glory,
Revive us again.

William P. Mackay (1839-1885)

Revive Us Again

[*Crusader Hymns,* No. 156]

A Hymn Story by Cliff Barrows

"Revive Us Again" is a gospel song that we have used in almost every evangelistic crusade since 1946. When we sing it, we often revert to the ancient practice of *antiphony* which was common in the performance of the Hebrew psalms. In the refrain, the audience on one side of the auditorium or stadium will sing "Hallelujah!" and those on the other side will echo "Thine the glory," and so on until the final phrase "Revive us again," which we sing in unison.

There are technical problems, of course! Because of the size of the congregations and the relatively slow speed at which sound travels, it is sometimes difficult to stay together. Nevertheless, even without the help of organ and piano, it is a thrilling experience of praise in song.

Sometimes we have sung the hymn responsively over long distances. In our final meeting in Sydney, Australia in 1959, the first phrase was sung by 80,000 people in the Royal Agriculture Society's Showground. They were answered by 70,000 people in the Cricket Ground, almost two blocks away. In 1955, by use of a telephone line relay, the folk in Bangor, North Wales responded to the audience in Glasgow, Scotland.

A critic of hymns might point out that the text of this poem is a bit incongruous. It first appeared in 1875 under the scripture verse, "O Lord, revive Thy work" (Hab. 3:2). The reader's initial reaction is that it is a prayer for spiritual revival among God's people. Nevertheless, the first three stanzas consist entirely of praising God. Only the last stanza seems to conform to the thought of the title, and is a prayer that the Church and each Christian in it might be renewed in faith and spiritual vigor. In the same way, the refrain echoes its paeans of praise over and over, and at the end—almost as an afterthought—there is the prayer "Revive us again."

We can be sure, however, that the author, William P. Mackay (a physician who became a Scottish Presbyterian minister), knew what he was doing. There is deep spiritual insight shown here, and we are reminded of the experience of the Israelites during the reign of Jehoshaphat (ca. 896 B.C.)

God's chosen people were being threatened by the Moabites and the Ammonites, and they were very much afraid. A word of encouragement was brought to King Jehoshaphat by Jahaziel, one of the musicians in the temple:

> **Thus saith the Lord unto you, Be not afraid nor dismayed by reason of this great multitude; for this battle is not yours, but God's . . . Ye shall not need to fight in this battle: set yourselves, stand ye still, and see the salvation of the Lord with you (II Chron. 20:15), 17).**

The story goes on:

> **And when he (Jehoshaphat) had consulted with the people, he appointed singers unto the Lord, and that should praise the beauty of holiness, as they went out before the army, and to say, Praise the Lord; for his mercy endureth forever.**
>
> **And when they began to sing and to praise, the Lord set ambushments against the children of Ammon, Moab, and mount Seir, which were come against Judah; and they were smitten (II Chron. 20:21, 22).**

The enemies of our souls are many, and we are often painfully aware of them — our own innate weaknesses, the world of allurements around us, and the Devil, who appears sometimes as a "roaring lion" and sometimes as an "angel of light." Our potential for victory against these foes will not be found within ourselves; it is not even the result of our own holy desires. The source of our victory is found in God, and our resources are His own divine holiness and power.

When we are properly conscious of God's attributes — as well as of our own weakness and vulnerability — and when we give Him glory, then His strength works through us. If you face a particularly heavy burden or a strong temptation today, lay it aside and sing a song of praise to God. "Revive Us Again" would be a good choice!

[Read or sing the entire hymn.]

Now Thank We All Our God

[*Crusader Hymns*, No. 256]

[Read or sing stanza 1.]

Many of our Christian songs have been forged in the heat of dramatic and moving experience. One reason for publishing *Crusade Hymn Stories* is the conviction that, if we know the circumstances connected with a hymn's writing, we may better understand its message.

On the other hand, the text of a hymn itself may give us an inkling about the life and work of its writer. For instance, the chorale "A Mighty Fortress" reveals the cataclysmic struggle between God and satanic powers, which parallels Martin Luther's crusade against the entrenched and decadent ecclesiastics of the 16th century. Another hymn like Rinkart's "Now Thank We All Our God" may seem to have little connection with the period and the situation in which it was produced. Investigation into its history turns up amazing facts.

Martin Rinkart was a pastor at Eilenberg, Saxony during the Thirty Years' War (1618-1648). Because Eilenberg was a walled city, it became a severely overcrowded refuge for political and military fugitives from far and near. As a result, the entire city suffered from famine and disease. In 1637 a great pestilence swept through the area, resulting in the death of some eight thousand persons, including Rinkart's wife. At that time he was the only minister in Eilenberg because the others had either died or fled. Rinkart alone conducted the burial services for 4480 people, sometimes as many as 40 or 50 a day!

During the closing years of the war, Eilenberg was overrun or besieged three times, once by the Austrian army and twice by the Swedes. On one occasion, the Swedish general demanded that the townspeople make a payment of 30,000 thalers. Martin Rinkart served as intermediary, pleading that the impoverished city could not meet such a levy; however, his request was disregarded. Turning to his companions the pastor said, "Come, my children, we can find no mercy with man; let us take refuge with God." On his knees he led them in a fervent prayer and in the singing of a familiar hymn, "When in the hour of utmost need." The Swedish commander was so moved that he reduced the levy to 1350 thalers.

We may well ask why all this dramatic experience and difficulty is not reflected in Rinkart's hymn. Had the good pastor seen so much stark tragedy that he had become insensitive to human needs and problems? Of course not. He simply had come to believe that God's providence is always good, no matter how much we are tempted to doubt it.

One of the Christian's favorite, often-quoted Bible verses is Romans 8:28 *(Living Letters):* "And we know that all that happens to us is working for our good if we love God, and if we are fitting into His plans." Do we really believe this assurance? In our testimonies and prayers, and even in some of the songs we sing, we seem to enjoy talking about our little troubles and difficulties, multiplying and magnifying them. We almost sound at times like "spiritual hypochondriacs!"

Actually, there is some hint of trouble in Rinkart's hymn. In the second stanza he asks that God will "guide us when perplexed, and free us from all ills." But the overwhelming atmosphere of the hymn breathes utter confidence in God, regardless of consequences. In fact, the last stanza is his own version of the *Gloria Patri* which many congregations sing every Sunday:

Glory be to the Father,
And to the Son, and to the Holy Ghost!
As it was in the beginning, is now and ever shall be,
World without end. Amen!

[Read or sing stanzas 2 and 3.]

In the nuclear world of tomorrow, it is entirely possible that we may experience great difficulty, persecution, and even war and death. Christians should prepare themselves and their families for this possibility, so that if and when it comes, we might face it in spiritual victory, giving testimony that ours is a faith that works. It may help us to know Martin Rinkart's experience and his hymn, which confirms these words of the Apostle Paul:

What can separate us from the love of Christ? Can affliction or hardship? Can persecution, hunger, nakedness, peril, or the sword? "We are being done to death for thy sake all day long," as Scripture says; "we have been treated like sheep for slaughter"—and yet, in spite of all, overwhelming victory is ours through him who loved us. For I am convinced that there is nothing in death or life, in the realm of spirits or superhuman powers, in the world as it is or the world as it shall be, in the forces of the universe, in heights or depths — nothing in all creation that can separate us from the love of God in Christ Jesus our Lord (Rom. 8:35-39, *New English Bible*).

Now thank we all our God
With heart and hands and voices,
Who wondrous things hath done,
In whom His world rejoices;
Who, from our mother's arms,
Hath blessed us on our way
With countless gifts of love,
And still is ours today.

O may this bounteous God
Through all our life be near us,
With ever joyful hearts
And blessed peace to cheer us;
And keep us in His grace,
And guide us when perplexed,
And free us from all ills
In this world and the next.

All praise and thanks to God
The Father now be given,
The Son, and Him who reigns
With them in highest heaven,
The one eternal God,
Whom earth and heaven adore;
For thus it was, is now,
And shall be evermore.

Martin Rinkart (1586-1649)
Tr. by Catherine Winkworth (1827-1878)

I have a song that Jesus gave me,
It was sent from heaven above;
There never was a sweeter melody,
'Tis a melody of love.

I love the Christ who died on Calvary,
For He washed my sins away;
He put within my heart a melody,
And I know it's there to stay.

'Twill be my endless theme in glory,
With the angels I will sing;
'Twill be a song with glorious harmony,
When the courts of heaven ring.

Refrain:

In my heart there rings a melody,
There rings a melody with heaven's harmony;
In my heart there rings a melody;
There rings a melody of love.

Elton M. Roth (1891-1951)

In My Heart There Rings a Melody

[*Crusader Hymns*, No. 105]

A Hymn Story by Tedd Smith

Not many people are given a great singing voice, but everyone can have a song! The Psalmist explains the source of the music in a Christian's life:

> **I waited patiently for the Lord: and he inclined unto me, and heard my cry. He brought me up also out of an horrible pit, out of the miry clay, and set my feet upon a rock, and established my goings. And he hath put a new song in my mouth, even praise unto our God: many shall see it, and fear, and shall trust in the Lord (Psalm 40:1-3).**

This new song which God gives us may have no words whatever, no melody, no rhythm and no harmony! This is a "song in the heart." The hymn title says "In my heart there rings a melody;" it is based on the words of the apostle Paul in Ephesians 5:19: "singing and making melody *in your heart* to the Lord."
[Read or sing stanza 1.]

What is the heart singing? The final phrase of the refrain describes it: it is a "melody of love" – God's love to us, and our love to God and to other men. It is a song of joy – not merely happiness or pleasure, but an eternal joy that persists through all the sorrows and tragedies of life. It is also a song of peace and serenity that gives poise and maturity amid the pressures of our culture.

Someone has said, "If there were more singing Christians, there would be more Christians!" If this heart-song of love, joy and peace is evident in our daily lives, we will become very conspicuous in our communities and in our daily life-contacts. Others will want to know the secret of our victorious living. As the Psalmist declared in the passage quoted previously, "many shall see it, and fear, and shall trust in the Lord."

Elton Menno Roth, the hymn's writer, was for many years a distinguished church musician – singer, composer and conductor. In the 1930's, after serious study with several prominent teachers, he organized professional choirs which achieved national recognition in their concert tours.

Roth once said that this hymn was written while he was conducting an evangelistic meeting in Texas. As he recalls:

> **One hot summer afternoon I took a little walk to the cotton mill just outside of town. On my way back through the burning streets of this typical plantation village, I became weary with the oppressive heat, and paused at a church on the corner.**
>
> **The door being open, I went in. There were no people in the pews, no minister in the pulpit. Everything was quiet, with a lingering sacred presence. I walked up and down the aisle and began singing, "In my heart there rings a melody," then hurried into the pastor's study to find some paper. I drew a staff and sketched the melody, remaining there for an hour or more to finish the song, both words and music.**
>
> **That evening I introduced it by having over two hundred boys and girls sing it at the open air meeting; after which the audience joined in the singing. I was thrilled as it seemed my whole being was transformed into a song!**

In my profession of church music, we hear a good deal of talk about the music which pleases God and which ministers to people. Like Roth, we must be concerned about the quality of our musical compositions, and our performance of them. But we dare not forget that God is more concerned about whether or not we have a song in our heart. It is this melody in a life which will convince other men and women that our Christian faith is vital and desirable.

[Read or sing stanzas 2 and 3.]

Trusting Jesus

[*Crusader Hymns*, No. 183]

A Hymn Story by Billy Graham

"Trusting Jesus" is a hymn that is completely American in background. Edgar Stites, author of the words, was a direct descendant of John Howland, one of the *Mayflower's* passengers. Active in the Civil War, he was later a riverboat pilot and then a missionary to the frontier churches in South Dakota.

The hymn poem first appeared in a newspaper, and was handed to the American evangelist D. L. Moody. In turn, Moody gave it to his soloist and songleader, Ira D. Sankey, asking him to set it to music. In his book, *Sankey's Story of the Gospel Hymns*, the singer says, "I assented, on condition that he should vouch for the doctrine taught in the verses, and he said he would."

This hymn was the favorite of my longtime friend, Dr. W. B. Riley, and it expresses well the motivating purpose of his life. During the more than forty years that Dr. Riley was the beloved pastor of the First Baptist Church in Minneapolis, Minnesota, he was a pillar of strength in the evangelical movement. He appeared many times at the Florida Bible Institute while I was a student there. He—and other men like Dr. H. H. Savage, Dr. William Evans and Dr. Vance Havner—instilled in me a love for the Word of God, and gave me my first doctrinal anchorage.

The frequent theme of Dr. Riley's preaching was the grace of God. He both taught and lived a practical Christianity that is proclaimed in this motto and title: "Trusting Jesus, That Is All."

[Read or sing stanzas 1 and 2.]

I have often emphasized that becoming a Christian is more than "making a decision" to live a better life or to attend church more regularly. When by faith we accept Christ as our Lord and Saviour, something supernatural takes place. He comes to dwell in our hearts, and gives us His own supernatural life—eternal life.

But it would be a mistake to imagine that from then on, we are automatically and almost magically victorious over sin and doubt. Not so! Each day we must have the same trust we experienced when we first came to know Christ. We all remember the words in Ephesians 2:8, "For by grace are ye saved through faith." But too many people forget Hebrews 10:38, "Now the just shall *live* by faith." This is the secret of *living* the Christian life – everyday faith – "simply trusting every day."

Each day we renew our faith in God's forgiveness. Sometimes after years of walking with God, the devil will tempt us to doubt our salvation. But on the strength of God's Word we can exercise faith and trust and drive the sin of doubt away.

We "simply trust" that God will keep us, guide us and protect us each day. It is probably a good thing that we know "not what a day may bring forth" (Prov. 27:1). For if we were to see the road ahead for the next month, or year, or ten years, we would probably not have the courage to face it.

The author Robert Louis Stevenson once said, "Every man can win through until nightfall." The Christian would agree, "Yes – with the consciousness that I am God's and He is mine!" God has not promised strength or grace or faith for tomorrow. He has said, "As thy days, so shall thy strength be" (Deut. 33:25).

If we use our resources of prayer, of God's Word, and of Christian fellowship – and if we exercise faith and trust for each day – we can live daily in glorious victory!

[Read or sing stanzas 3 and 4.]

Simply trusting every day,
Trusting through a stormy way;
Even when my faith is small,
Trusting Jesus, that is all.

Brightly doth His Spirit shine
Into this poor heart of mine;
While He leads I cannot fall;
Trusting Jesus, that is all.

Singing if my way is clear;
Praying if the path be drear;
If in danger, for Him call;
Trusting Jesus, that is all.

Trusting Him while life shall last,
Trusting Him till earth be past;
Till within the jasper wall:
Trusting Jesus, that is all.

Refrain:

Trusting as the moments fly,
Trusting as the days go by;
Trusting Him whate'er befall,
Trusting Jesus, that is all.

Edgar P. Stites (1836-1921)

Immortal, invisible, God only wise,
    In light inaccessible hid from our eyes,
Most blessed, most glorious, the Ancient of Days,
    Almighty, victorious, Thy great name we praise.

Unresting, unhasting, and silent as light,
    Nor wanting, nor wasting, Thou rulest in might;
Thy justice like mountains high soaring above
    Thy clouds, which are fountains of goodness and love.

To all, life Thou givest, to both great and small,
    In all life Thou livest, the true life of all,
We blossom and flourish as leaves on the tree,
    And wither and perish — but nought changeth Thee.

Great Father of glory, pure Father of light,
    Thine angels adore Thee, all veiling their sight;
All praise we would render; O help us to see
    'Tis only the splendor of light hideth Thee!

Walter Chalmers Smith (1824-1908)

Immortal, Invisible, God Only Wise

[*Crusader Hymns*, No. 43]

Have you ever tried to look at the sun? "Of course not," you say. "If I tried it even for a few moments, it would damage my eyes. This is why, to view an eclipse of the sun, I must look through a very dark lens." Isn't it interesting that the sun is obscured by the very light which it produces? The hymn "Immortal, Invisible, God Only Wise" says that this is one of the reasons why it is difficult to "see God" — to understand Him.
[Read or sing stanza 1.]

The Bible often speaks of God as "light." David said, "The Lord is my light and my salvation" (Psalm 27:1). Jesus himself stated, "I am the light of the world" (John 8:12). One of Jesus' disciples wrote, "God is light, and in him is no darkness at all" (I John 1:5).

Notice, in this hymn of worship, the many ways in which God is compared to the light of the sun. In stanza two, we are reminded that God never rests, never hurries. Despite all His power, God acts so quietly in the universe that those who are "spiritually blind" never perceive him. This anonymity is why it is possible for some ecclesiastic leaders to propose that God may be dead.

Like the sun, God needs nothing for sustenance; all things depend upon Him. Like the sun, God's power never diminishes; He is immutable, never changing. In a world of turmoil and incessant change, we can count on His eternal "justice, goodness and love."

Just as physical life depends upon the sun, so all life — physical and spiritual — depends upon God. Through the chemical phenomenon we call photosynthesis, plants derive food from the energy of the sun. We in turn obtain our nourishment from plants and from animals which live on plants. Yes, God uses light — physical and spiritual light — to give physical and spiritual life "to both great and small." This is why Jesus said: "I am the light of the world: he that followeth me shall not walk in darkness, but shall have the light of life" (John 8:12).

Revelation 21:23 promises that heaven's inhabitants will need neither a sun nor a moon, "for the glory of God did lighten it, and the Lamb (Christ) is the light thereof." Another passage of scripture (Isaiah 6:2) suggests that the angels cover their eyes because they cannot stand the brightness of His glory. If, while we are still mortal, we fail to fully comprehend God, we must remember that the light of the sun is what makes it invisible. So we sing to Him in humble praise: "Only the splendor of light hideth Thee!"

It is foolish to think that we dare not believe in a God we cannot completely understand. We are confident that there is an earthly plane of existence although we don't entirely comprehend it. The real wonder for us to ponder is that this transcendent being comes to dwell in our hearts if we invite Him. Scripture verifies this truth:

> **For thus saith the high and lofty One that inhabiteth eternity, whose name is Holy; I dwell in the high and holy place, with him also that is of a contrite and humble spirit (Isa. 57:15).**

Frederick Faber expresses this paradox of man's finiteness indwelt by Divine infinity, in a hymn of his own:

My God, how wonderful Thou art,
Thy majesty how bright!
How beautiful Thy mercy seat,
In depths of burning light!

O how I fear thee, living God,
With deepest, tend'rest fears;
And worship Thee with trembling hope,
And penitential tears.

Yet I may love Thee too, O Lord,
Almighty as Thou art;
For Thou hast stooped to ask of me
The love of my poor heart.

"Immortal, Invisible, God Only Wise" was written by Walter Chalmers Smith (1824-1908) who was a pastor and once moderator of the Free Church of Scotland (Presbyterian).

As you sing or read this hymn, notice that its opening phrase is a paean of praise appropriated from I Timothy 1:17: "Now unto the King eternal, immortal, invisible, the only wise God, be honour and glory forever and ever."

[Read or sing stanzas 2-4.]

He the Pearly Gates Will Open

[*Crusader Hymns*, No. 250]

A Hymn Story by Cliff Barrows

In preparation for a series of crusade services in Scandinavia in 1955, we were looking for something in simple Swedish to sing. Someone suggested "Han skall öppna pärleporten," in translation, "He the Pearly Gates Will Open." Because the song is a "natural" duet, Bev Shea graciously asked me to sing it with him. It is one of the two or three songs we sing together on rare occasions, and we have repeated it for the Danes in Copenhagen and for the American Swedes in places like Rockford, Illinois and Minneapolis, Minnesota.

Elsie Ahlwen, composer of this lovely tune, came to America from Sweden and became a student at the Moody Bible Institute. After graduation she began to work among the Swedish immigrants in Chicago, and later became a full-time evangelist. The words of this refrain had been known to her for a long time, and she often sang it to her own melody in evangelistic services throughout the country. It came to be the theme song of Elsie Ahlwen's ministry.

During a meeting in Chicago, Miss Ahlwen was approached by an old man who gave her the words for the stanzas. They had been written by Fred Blom, a former Christian worker in Sweden. Blom had come to New York early in this century, and, through circumstances that are not quite clear, had fallen into sin and was sent to prison. It was there, sick in soul and in body, that he found Christ anew. The song was his expression of joy because God had "healed his backsliding" and forgiven all his sin.

In keeping with the immigrant background of the song, it must be noted that the original was in the Swedish tongue. Not until the time of a great revival in Duluth, Minnesota was this hymn first translated into English. "He the Pearly Gates Will Open" has now been rendered in more than a dozen languages.

Before hearing this hymn story, I had always wondered just what was behind the words of the second stanza:

Like a dove when hunted, frightened,
As a wounded fawn was I;
Broken hearted, yet He healed me—
He will heed the sinner's cry.

This was Fred Blom's experience. At one time he had known God's peace and victory over sin, but he had fallen victim to the temptations of this world. Yet the love of Christ would not let him go. It pursued him relentlessly — almost as a hunter stalks a deer — and finally the arrow of conviction brought him down. We are reminded of the words of David in Psalm 38:1,2: "O Lord, rebuke me not in thy wrath: neither chasten me in thy hot displeasure. For thine arrows stick fast in me, and thy hand presseth me sore."

It is always tragic when a Christian falls into sin because he loses his sweet fellowship with God and compromises his witness for Christ. Yet all of us have failed at one time or another. We may not have committed some grossly evil act, but we have "fallen short" in word or thought or deed. Perhaps we have failed to do some deed of kindness, or to show love and concern for others. How wonderful to know that God "is married to the backslider" (Jer. 3:14). He will not allow us to be comfortable in our failure. Still His love follows us — sometimes it is shown in trouble and affliction — until we come to our senses and return to Him.

The hymn's message is very simple. Because of the love of God expressed in Christ our sins are forgiven, our lives are changed, and we anticipate a joyful entrance into heaven. It is said that Fred Blom died in the custody of the law. While the gates of prison did not open for him, he knew that heaven's "pearly gates" would be swung wide by his Redeemer.

Elsie Ahlwen's personal testimony voices the same assurance. She had married Daniel A. Sundeen, a business man, and they had continued a ministry together while raising their family. In 1962, they visited Chicago once again and sang "Pearly Gates" for their many friends. Shortly thereafter, Mr. Sundeen took sick and died within a week. Mrs. Sundeen wrote these words: "It is difficult to see beyond the bend in the road where your loved one disappeared. But how good it is to know that, when my Lord calls me, the Pearl Gates will open — not because of my worthiness but because He purchased my salvation."
[Read or sing the entire hymn.]

Love divine, so great and wondrous,
Deep and mighty, pure, sublime;
Coming from the heart of Jesus –
Just the same through tests of time.

Like a dove when hunted, frightened,
As a wounded fawn was I;
Broken hearted, yet He healed me –
He will heed the sinner's cry.

Love divine, so great and wondrous –
All my sins He then forgave,
I will sing His praise forever,
For His blood, His pow'r to save.

In life's eventide, at twilight,
At His door I'll knock and wait;
By the precious love of Jesus
I shall enter heaven's gate.

Refrain:

He the pearly gates will open,
So that I may enter in;
For He purchased my redemption,
And forgave me all my sin.

Fred Blom (20th Century)
Trans. by N. Carlson (1879-1957)

When all my labors and trials are o'er,
And I am safe on that beautiful shore,
Just to be near the dear Lord I adore,
Will through the ages be glory for me.

When by the gift of His infinite grace,
I am accorded in heaven a place,
Just to be there and to look on His face,
Will through the ages be glory for me.

Friends will be there I have loved long ago;
Joy like a river around me will flow;
Yet, just a smile from my Saviour, I know,
Will through the ages be glory for me.

Refrain:

O that will be glory for me,
Glory for me, glory for me;
When by His grace I shall look on His face,
That will be glory, be glory for me.

Charles H. Gabriel (1856-1932)

O That Will Be Glory

[*Crusader Hymns*, No. 252]

A Hymn Story by Cliff Barrows

It is often difficult to predict whether or not a new hymn will "catch on" with the public. Actually, only a small number of those that are published ever reach a second edition. Of the 6500 hymns written by Charles Wesley during the 18th century, probably no more than 200 are sung anywhere today. The new *Methodist Hymnal* (1964), compiled by Americans of the Wesleyan tradition, contains only 79 of Charles Wesley's hymns. Even so, this is a remarkable record of poetic longevity that is not equaled by any other hymnwriter.

When "O That Will Be Glory" first appeared in 1900, a musical expert predicted, "It will never go. It has too many quarter notes." In other words, "the rhythm is too monotonous." But in a few years, it was the most popular hymn Homer Rodeheaver led in the Billy Sunday campaigns. It was affectionately called the "Glory Song" and was inspired, not by an experience, but by a personality!

The author, C. H. Gabriel, was perhaps the best known and most prolific gospel song writer of the early twentieth century. One of his good friends was Ed Card, superintendent of the Sunshine Rescue Mission of St. Louis, Missouri. Ed was a radiant believer who always seemed to be "bubbling over" with Christian joy. During a sermon or a prayer he would often explode with "Glory!" just as some people say "Amen!" or "Hallelujah!" His beaming smile earned him the nickname "old glory face." It was his custom to close his fervent prayers with a reference to heaven, usually ending with the phrase "and that will be glory for me!"

[Read or sing stanza 1.]

No doubt many Christians have a false view of what heaven will be. Our critics often say that we yearn for "pie in the sky by and by," while failing to really confront the issues that face us here and now. It is true that heaven will be free of the sorrow and death, the pressures and conflicts which beset us on earth. But it is not a truly Christian motive to look for heaven simply because we will have no problems there.

Many folks have a similar misconception of what the Bible calls "eternal life," imagining that this is the life which begins when we die or when Christ returns to this earth. "Eternal" life means a new *quality* of life — a supernatural life which begins when we enter God's family. The Bible says it clearly: "And what is it God has said? That He has given us eternal life, and that this life is in His Son. So whoever has God's Son has life; whoever does not have His Son, does not have life" (I John 5:11,12, *Living Letters*). We believe that heaven is really a continuation of that eternal life which we may possess right now.

At the same time, one of the delightful prospects of eternity is that we will be able to accomplish the things which are, for one reason or another, impossible in this world. For one thing, we will have new bodies which will not be limited by time or space. We believe also that many of the "mysteries of our faith" — mysteries because of our mental limitations — will then be made clear. We expect that we will gain victory over all our doubts and over the sinful weaknesses which plague us now. Some people contend that it is possible that we will continue to grow mentally and spiritually through all eternity. Furthermore, it is reasonable to anticipate that in heaven God will have service for us to perform, although the Bible does not specifically list our responsibilities.

I have heard some people say that they expect to be musical experts in heaven, although they have little musical talent now. It is true that we will all be able to sing the anthem mentioned in Revelation 5:12: "Worthy is the Lamb that was slain to receive power, and riches, and wisdom, and strength, and honour, and glory, and blessing."

What this "Glory Song" really says is that the central attraction in heaven will be Jesus Christ. We will see Him then "in His completeness, face to face," not "as if we were peering at His reflection in a poor mirror" (I Cor. 13:12, *LL*). And all the changes that will take place in us will happen because "when He comes we will be like Him, as a result of seeing Him as He really is" (I John 3:2, *LL*).

I shall see Him, I shall be like Him,
By one glance of His face transformed;
And this body of sin and darkness
To the image of Christ conformed. (A. J. Gordon)

[Read or sing stanzas 2 and 3.]

For the Beauty of the Earth

[*Crusader Hymns*, No. 18]

A Hymn Story by Don Hustad

Suppose you were to visit a great artist in his studio, and all around you the walls were covered by his paintings. Is it possible that you might ignore all the beauty that he had created, and never once mention it?

Some of us treat God's artistry this way! Our heavenly Father is the Creator and Giver of all that is beautiful in the universe. The first chapter of Genesis tells us that God approved of all His handiwork, repeating several times "and God saw that it was good." Undoubtedly He is pleased when we recognize the beauty of our world and thank Him for it. Yes, a Christian does have an obligation with regard to beauty. "Whatsoever things are true, whatsoever things are honest... just... pure... lovely... of good report... think on these things" (Phil. 4:8).

There are many other aspects of our world which we take for granted: health, homes, friends, our country, even life itself. The hymn "For the Beauty of the Earth" lists some of God's blessings for which we may seem to be ungrateful. Do we feel that these are "secular" aspects of life, and that we should limit our praying and singing to "spiritual" things? Yet all of these so-called "ordinary" things are the gifts of God. We should thank Him for them!
[Read or sing stanzas 1 and 2.]

The late Dr. A. W. Tozer once said that every artist's work is in a sense "praise of God." The painter, the sculptor, and the musician are simply imitating God's own magnificent creative acts, using the talents which God has given them. For this reason, the Christian also sees the hand of God in all good art.

Not only did God put beautiful sounds and sights in the world — He also gave us ears and eyes to take them in, and minds to interpret what we hear and see. It is proper to thank God for a clear mind and the joy we find in developing it through study or in research. This too is His great gift to us and our gratitude is expressed in a stanza which is not always included in hymnals:

For the joy of ear and eye,
For the heart and mind's delight,
For the mystic harmony
Linking sense to sound and sight:
Lord of all, to Thee we raise
This our hymn of grateful praise.

In the remaining stanzas, author Folliott S. Pierpoint gives thanks for all human relationships, whether of family or of friends, and for the fellowship of the Christian church encircling the world. A final verse, omitted in most books, gives thanks for God Himself, who has given us all the joys and beauty of life—but more than all this, "His only begotten Son."

For Thyself, best Gift Divine!
To our race so freely given;
For that great, great love of Thine,
Peace on earth, and joy in heaven:
Lord of all, to Thee we raise
This our hymn of grateful praise.

When this hymn was first sung, the final phrase was:

Christ, our God, to Thee we raise
This our sacrifice of praise.

Perhaps the present version sings better but it omits an important truth about church music. Throughout the Bible, singing is often spoken of as a "sacrifice"—a "sacrifice of joy" or a "sacrifice of praise." Hebrews 13:15 states this challenge: "By him *(Jesus Christ)* therefore let us offer the sacrifice of praise to God continually, that is, the fruit of our lips giving thanks to his name."

God wants nothing more than our praise, our worship. A "sacrifice" is something which costs the giver a great deal. I have often encouraged songleaders and ministers of music to challenge Christian believers to really exert themselves, both physically and mentally, when they sing. One of Charles Wesley's hymns wishes for a "thousand tongues to sing my great Redeemer's praise." We should at least use the one we have, to full advantage!

What shall I render unto the Lord for all his benefits toward me? . . . I will offer . . . the sacrifice of thanksgiving, and will call upon the name of the Lord (Psalm 116:12, 17).

[Read or sing stanzas 3 and 4.]

For the beauty of the earth,
For the glory of the skies,
For the love which from our birth
Over and around us lies,
Lord of all, to Thee we raise
This our hymn of grateful praise.

For the beauty of each hour
Of the day and of the night,
Hill and vale, and tree, and flower,
Sun and moon, and stars of light,
Lord of all, to Thee we raise
This our hymn of grateful praise.

For the joy of human love,
Brother, sister, parent, child,
Friends on earth, and friends above,
For all gentle thoughts and mild,
Lord of all, to Thee we raise
This our hymn of grateful praise.

For Thy Church that evermore
Lifteth holy hands above,
Offering up on every shore
Her pure sacrifice of love,
Lord of all, to Thee we raise
This our hymn of grateful praise.

Folliott S. Pierpoint (1835-1917)

O come, O come, Emmanuel,
    And ransom captive Israel,
That mourns in lonely exile here
    Until the Son of God appear.
Rejoice! rejoice! Emmanuel
    Shall come to thee, O Israel!

O come, Thou Rod of Jesse, free
    Thine own from Satan's tyranny;
From depths of hell Thy people save
    And give them victory o'er the grave.
Rejoice! rejoice! Emmanuel
    Shall come to thee, O Israel!

O come, Thou Day-spring, come and cheer
    Our spirits by Thine advent here;
And drive away the shades of night,
    And pierce the clouds and bring us light!
Rejoice! rejoice! Emmanuel
    Shall come to thee, O Israel!

O come, Thou Key of David, come,
    And open wide our heavenly home;
Make safe the way that leads on high,
    And close the path to misery.
Rejoice! Rejoice! Emmanuel
    Shall come to thee, O Israel!

Latin Hymn, ca. 9th Century
Tr. by John Mason Neale (1818-1866)

O Come, O Come, Emmanuel

[*Crusader Hymns*, No. 262]

Like Topsy in the story *Uncle Tom's Cabin*, some of our hymns were not specifically composed; they "just growed." The song "O Come, O Come, Emmanuel" evolved in this way.

This Advent hymn began to take shape more than a thousand years ago. In a series of seven Vesper services preceding Christmas, church choirs traditionally sang each night a different verse (or Antiphon) addressed to Christ. Three hundred years later these separate verses were united, a refrain was added, and the result was a hymn. About one hundred years ago the hymn was translated from Latin into English, and it is just now becoming known to many Christian congregations.

"O Come, O Come, Emmanuel" is a prayer that anticipates the coming of Christ to this earth. His coming as the Messiah ("deliverer") was first prophesied in the sixth century B.C., when the Jews were captive in Babylon. For centuries thereafter, faithful Hebrews looked for their Messiah with great longing and expectation, echoing the prayer that he would "ransom captive Israel." Indeed, many Jews are still looking for a Messiah, because they have failed to recognize Jesus as the Promised One.

Jesus Christ the Redeemer, capstone of man's longing through the ages, is addressed in the first stanza of this hymn as "Emmanuel." The words of Matthew 1:23 corroborate the prophecy in Isaiah 7:14, "Behold a virgin shall be with child, and shall bring forth a son, and they shall call his name Emmanuel, which being interpreted is, God with us."
[Read or sing stanza 1.]

Another title used in the song to refer to Jesus is "Thou Rod of Jesse." The source of this symbolism is Isaiah 11:1, "And there shall come forth a rod out of the stem of Jesse, and a Branch shall grow out of his roots." This particular prophecy was fulfilled by the birth of Jesus, whose heritage stemmed from the kingly line of David, the son of Jesse. But, contrary to the Jews' expectation, the purpose of Christ's first coming was not to restore their kingdom or to bring them political freedom. He came rather to free "all who will believe" from the tyranny

of Satan, from hell and the grave. Ultimately, when Christ comes again He will indeed rule as absolute King over the universe.
[Read or sing stanza 2.]

"The Dayspring" is the vivid image applied to Jesus in the third stanza; it means literally "sun rising." Jesus' birth had been prophesied shortly before the event by the priest Zacharias, in these words: "The dayspring from on high hath visited us, to give light to them that sit in darkness and in the shadow of death" (Luke 1:78b, 79a). Christ's coming into the world is thus likened to the sun breaking on the horizon after a long dark night.
[Read or sing stanza 3.]

The final stanza again mentions the prophetic aspect of Christ's advent; He is called "Thou Key of David." This reference is first recorded in Isaiah 22:22, "and the key of the house of David will I lay upon his shoulder." These words remind us that in Oriental countries, keys were a symbol of authority and were sometimes worn hanging from the shoulder. Another well-known passage confirms this royal authority of Christ, "and the government shall be upon his shoulder" (Isa. 9:6).

The spiritual significance of "Christ the Key" is vividly demonstrated to modern-day visitors to the Near East. In Nablus, Jordan there is an old Samaritan synagogue that welcomes tourists. A bearded priest takes out three brass keys and opens three locks to let the visitors into the "holy place." In the hymn, however, the "key" is Christ who opens the entrance to God; keys of brass are no longer needed. When Christ died and His deed of redemption was finished on Golgotha, the veil before the "holy place" in the temple was rent. He, "the key," opened up the way to God for all.

From beginning to end, all the stanzas of the hymn remind us of Christ's first advent and project our attention to His second coming. Expectation must necessarily be a part of the Christian's life. The real home of the believer is with Christ in heaven; here on earth he is, in a sense, an exile. One day, like a glorious sunrise, Christ will "pierce the clouds" and bring us final and total victory over death.

The hymn's title is similar to the words of the next-to-the-last verse of the Bible: "Even so, come, Lord Jesus." And we can joyfully echo the refrain: "Rejoice! rejoice! Emmanuel shall come!"
[Read or sing stanza 4.]

Awake, My Soul, and with the Sun

[*Crusader Hymns*, No. 50]

A Hymn Story by Don Hustad

When Thomas Ken was a student in the cathedral school at Winchester, England in 1650, that institution was already nearly 300 years old! His day of classes, study and worship began at five o'clock in the morning; in the summer the sun was just breaking through, but in the winter it was still very dark. How hard it was to get out of their "truckle beds" in the cold dormitory, and then to participate in "morning prayers" and a hymn – all before breakfast. In those days, as had been the custom for those 300 years, the boys sang the Latin hymn *Jam lucis orto sidere*, "Now the daylight fills the sky."

A few years later, Ken returned to Winchester as a Fellow in the College and a member of the Cathedral staff. By this time English was largely replacing Latin for worship and the young teacher wrote a book of prayers and hymns for the boys to use. He added the recommendation that they "be sure to sing the morning and evening hymn in their chamber devoutly."

Ken's morning hymn began: "Awake, my soul, and with the sun thy daily stage of duty run." He must have remembered his own school days when he urged: "Shake off dull sloth, and joyful rise to pay thy morning sacrifice." All through the Old Testament, singing to God is called a "sacrifice of joy" or a "sacrifice of praise." This is one sacrifice which believers still offer to God. As we read in Hebrews 13:15, "By him (Jesus Christ) let us offer the sacrifice of praise to God continually, that is, the fruit of our lips giving thanks to his name."

Perhaps early morning is the very best time for us to worship God privately. Throughout the night, though we have been asleep, the angels have continued to praise God as the second stanza suggests. In Revelation 4:8, heavenly beings are spoken of who "rest not day and night, saying, Holy, holy, holy, Lord God Almighty, which was, and is, and is to come." Certainly it is appropriate that after we have rested through the night, we should join the angels in worship. Our first thoughts should be of our heavenly Father; our first conversation should be with Him.

We should also acknowledge, as does the third stanza, that God has cared for us through the night. The psalmist said of the Lord: "He that keepeth thee will not slumber." There are periods in the night and even through the day when our minds are not completely fixed on God. On my desk at home, I have a quotation Lord Astley made before the battle of Edgehill: "Lord, Thou knowest I shall be very busy this day. I may forget Thee. Do not Thou forget me." We may be assured that He never does forget us.

An early morning prayer, Bible reading and even a hymn can determine the quality of the entire day ahead. When we seek the face of God before we see other faces, even those of our own family, somehow the day is off to a better start.

As we pray, we should acknowledge that the new day is God's and that we are His *for this day.* We should echo Thomas Ken's petition made in the final stanza, that God shall "direct and control" all that we think or do or say, so that all our physical, mental and spiritual "powers might unite"—that is, might be focused and coordinated to the glory of God.

[Read or sing the entire hymn.]

My good friend, the Chinese evangelist Leland Wang, has long practiced the motto "No Bible, no breakfast." I am sure that he also meant "No prayer, no breakfast." May we be bold enough to add "No hymn of praise, no breakfast"? It may be difficult to really vocalize early in the morning without the lubrication of a cup of coffee. But we can at least repeat in our hearts the words of that other stanza given us by Thomas Ken. We call it the "Doxology:"

Praise God, from whom all blessings flow;
    Praise Him, all creatures here below;
Praise Him above, ye heavenly host;
    Praise Father, Son, and Holy Ghost.

Awake, my soul, and with the sun
    Thy daily stage of duty run;
Shake off dull sloth, and joyful rise
    To pay thy morning sacrifice.

Wake, and lift up thyself, my heart,
    And with the angels bear thy part,
Who all night long unwearied sing
    High praise to the Eternal King.

All praise to Thee, who safe hast kept,
    And hast refreshed me while I slept:
Grant, Lord, when I from death shall wake,
    I may of endless life partake.

Direct, control, suggest, this day,
    All I design, or do, or say;
That all my powers, with all their might,
    In Thy sole glory may unite.

Thomas Ken (1637-1711)

I will sing of my Redeemer
And His wondrous love to me;
On the cruel cross He suffered,
From the curse to set me free.

I will tell the wondrous story,
How my lost estate to save,
In His boundless love and mercy,
He the ransom freely gave.

I will praise my dear Redeemer,
His triumphant power I'll tell,
How the victory He giveth
Over sin, and death, and hell.

I will sing of my Redeemer
And His heavenly love for me;
He from death to life hath brought me,
Son of God, with Him to be.

Refrain:

Sing, oh, sing of my Redeemer,
With His blood He purchased me,
On the cross He sealed my pardon,
Paid the debt, and made me free.

Philip P. Bliss (1838-1876)

I Will Sing of My Redeemer

[*Crusader Hymns*, No. 93]

A Hymn Story by Cliff Barrows

Ninety years of world-wide popularity have established the gospel song "I Will Sing of My Redeemer" as part of our musical heritage. Less well known, however, is the miraculous legend of how it was preserved for the future. The composition was found in a piece of baggage rescued from a fiery train wreck on the day of December 20, 1876. The poem's author, 38-year-old Philip P. Bliss, had been traveling with his wife to Chicago to fulfill an engagement at D. L. Moody's Tabernacle. Near Ashtabula, Ohio a bridge collapsed and the train plunged into an icy river bed. It is said that Bliss survived the fall and climbed out through a coach window only to return, looking for his wife. Reunited, they died together in the flaming wreckage.

These circumstances, to all appearances, cut a brilliant career short, very suddenly. It had only been two years that Bliss had served as soloist and songleader in the evangelistic campaigns of Major D. W. Whittle. All his life, it would seem, had been leading up toward this ministry. Born in a log cabin, young Philip had left home at the age of eleven to work on farms and in lumber camps. He had become a Christian at the age of twelve and soon afterward developed interest in the study of music.

In the early nineteenth century, popular music training in America was centered in "singing schools"—schools which were characterized by a strong spiritual emphasis, and which also provided social activity for the small towns and rural communities. The "singing school" was strictly a one-man operation; a musician of some degree of ability traveled from place to place, organizing the classes, teaching them and collecting his fees (which might be paid either in cash or in farm produce!)

Most of the classes in sight-reading and in conducting were held at night. In the country schoolhouses, churches or town halls, the students sang the syllables (do-re-mi) while seated on planks placed between two chairs. Each music student also "beat time" for himself by moving his hand and arm in a prescribed pattern. Many of our early gospel musicians started out as "singing school" teachers. This tradition lasted more than a hundred years, and had a profound effect on the quality of congregational singing and the development of church choirs.

Philip Bliss found himself strongly attracted to "singing school" life. At the age of 21, he was married and a year later began a career as an itinerant music teacher. Using a little twenty-dollar folding organ hauled from place to place by his faithful horse Fanny, he taught music during the winter seasons. During the summer he followed his own musical education and became a student himself at the Normal Academy of Music at Geneseo, New York.

Song-writing came naturally to Bliss; he composed equally well in both words and music. Even during his short lifetime he was recognized as the leading writer of simple sacred songs, many of which are still widely used today. The new *Baptist Hymnal*, published in 1956, includes twelve hymns for which Bliss wrote either the words or the music, or both. Our small volume, *Crusader Hymns*, has seven of his compositions.

Although Bliss's ministry was very brief, his influence has continued down through the years. It was D. L. Moody who challenged him to leave teaching and to give his time to evangelistic crusades. In turn, Bliss urged his close friend and fellow-musician James McGranahan to undertake a similar task in gospel work. It was McGranahan who took Bliss's place in that fateful weekend meeting at the Moody Tabernacle in Chicago, when Bliss died enroute. At a later date, McGranahan joined the evangelistic party of D. W. Whittle.

We team musicians have been greatly inspired by the lives and contributions of these early evangelistic song leaders. And today—almost a century later—God still uses their simple songs and hymns to touch men's hearts, and to challenge many to decide for Christ.

God may not give each of us a great talent to use for Him. We may not have many years of service. But what we have—in talent and in time—is enough for God to bless and to use in accomplishing His purposes.

This song of Philip Bliss is a very simple expression of the truth of the gospel—so obvious that it does not require elaboration. In fact, the title itself might be considered the motto of his short and brilliant life: "I Will Sing of My Redeemer."

[Read or sing the entire hymn.]

Join All the Glorious Names

[*Crusader Hymns,* No. 17]

[Read or sing stanza 1]

The meaning of words may change drastically over a period of time. For this reason, it may take some effort to fully comprehend "Join All The Glorious Names," a 250-year-old hymn of Isaac Watts, even though some publishers have already made efforts to modernize it. For instance, the word "poor" in stanza 1 was originally "mean." (Try reading it that way.) The message of the hymn is basically this: all the names which have been given to Jesus Christ are altogether inadequate to express the glory of the character of this God-man.

Some of the most common names of Christ are mentioned in the five stanzas given here. The original hymn had seven more verses, but even these do not exhaust the titles given to our Lord. Jesus is often spoken of as "Prophet, Priest, and King." As prophet, He brought the good news of the gospel contained in such familiar passages as Luke 19:10, "The Son of man is come to seek and to save that which was lost;" and John 10:10, "I am come that they might have life, and that they might have it more abundantly."

A priest is one who represents the people before God. Hebrews 2:17 says of Christ, "Wherefore in all things it behooved him to be made like unto his brethren, that he might be a merciful and faithful high priest in things pertaining to God, to make reconciliation for the sins of the people." Jesus Himself *became* our "sacrifice for sin" when He died on the cross, and we believe that He continues to represent us at the throne of God. The third stanza suggests that it is Jesus' blood which pleads our cause. Another hymn (by Charles Wesley) speaks thus of the continuing priesthood of Christ:

Five bleeding wounds He bears,
Received on Calvary;
They pour effectual prayers,
They strongly plead for me;
"Forgive him, O forgive," they cry,
"Nor let that ransomed sinner die!"

[Read or sing stanzas 2 and 3.]

When the Jews looked for a "Messiah," they expected a powerful military and political figure. They rejected Jesus—and that name means "deliverer"—partly because they did not understand how this "lowly Nazarene" could liberate them from the power of Rome. We should not forget that Jesus came to be a "King." When Pilate asked Him, "Art thou a king then?" Jesus answered, "To this end was I born, and for this cause came I into the world" (John 18:37). Those of us who accept Christ as our Lord make him "King of our lives." Certainly, He is King of Heaven now, and there will come a day when He shall rule the earth as well, as an absolute Monarch. As we sing in Handel's *Messiah*, He shall be "King of Kings, and Lord of Lords, and shall reign forever and ever" (Rev. 19:16).

Some of the names of Christ were first spoken by prophets many years before Jesus' birth. Isaiah (9:6) says that "His name shall be called Wonderful, Counsellor, The mighty God, The everlasting Father, the Prince of Peace." Many of the poetic passages of the Old Testament psalms refer to the glory of Christ with such titles as "the Rose of Sharon" and the "lily of the valleys" (Song of Solomon 2:1). In the last book of the Bible, Jesus said, "I am the bright and morning star" (Rev. 22:16).

Other terms are used to speak of Christ's work in salvation. He is the "Lamb of God," "Saviour," "Redeemer," "Mediator" and "Emmanuel."

Of course, Jesus gave Himself many other descriptive names. He said: "I am the living bread which came down from heaven" (John 6:51). "I am the Good Shepherd" (John 10:14). "I am the Door" (John 10:9). "I am the light of the world" (John 8:12). "I am the true vine" (John 15:1). "I am the resurrection and the life" (John 11:25). These are just a few of the more than one hundred names of Christ which are found in the Bible.

Hymnwriters have also added new names to our Lord. Some of them are borrowed from scripture, with just a bit of poetic alteration: "The Son of Mary," "The Sun of Righteousness," "The Solid Rock," "Rock of Ages," "Blessed Redeemer," "Rod of Jesse," "Key of David," "Love Divine," "The Church's One Foundation," "Blessed Master," "High King of Heaven," "Heart of My Own Heart," "The Deep Sweet Well of Love," "Our Captain in the well-fought fight," "Risen, conquering Son," "Chief of ten thousand," "Fount of Every Blessing," "Friend for sinners," "Joy of Loving Hearts," "Prince of Glory," "Man of Sorrows," "Lover of my soul," and "My Guide and Keeper." (Suggestion: You might like to try to remember what hymns contain these phrases. They are all found in the book, *Crusader Hymns*.)

But we have not yet mentioned some of the most striking and significant names of Christ. He is the Son of God and the Son of Man. He said, "I am Alpha and Omega, the beginning and the end, the first and the last" (Rev. 22:13). He also said, "I am the Way, the Truth and the

Life" (John 14:6). No other sober and responsible person in the world's history ever uttered such audacious words!

It is obvious that all the names that might be invented would fail to adequately describe the character of our Lord. Yet writers and hymnists will no doubt continue to search for more. It is a good thing to express praise of Christ with such an expanded vocabulary. But more than this, we should praise Him with our daily lives and our willing service.

[Read or sing stanzas 4 and 5.]

Join all the glorious names
Of wisdom, love, and power,
That ever mortals knew,
That angels ever bore:
All are too poor to speak His worth,
Too poor to set my Saviour forth.

Great Prophet of my God,
My tongue would bless Thy name:
By Thee the joyful news
Of our salvation came,
The joyful news of sins forgiv'n,
Of hell subdued and peace with heav'n.

Jesus, my great High Priest,
Offered His blood, and died;
My guilty conscience seeks
No sacrifice beside:
His pow'rful blood did once atone
And now it pleads before the throne.

Thou art my Counsellor,
My Pattern, and my Guide,
And Thou my Shepherd art;
Oh, keep me near Thy side;
Nor let my feet e'er turn astray,
To wander in the crooked way.

My Saviour and my Lord,
My Conqueror and my King,
Thy sceptre and Thy sword,
Thy reigning grace I sing:
Thine is the pow'r; behold I sit
In willing bonds beneath Thy feet.

Isaac Watts (1674-1748)

Hark! the herald angels sing,
"Glory to the new-born King:
Peace on earth, and mercy mild,
God and sinners reconciled!"
Joyful, all ye nations, rise,
Join the triumph of the skies;
With th'angelic host proclaim,
"Christ is born in Bethlehem!"

Christ, by highest heaven adored;
Christ, the Everlasting Lord!
Late in time behold Him come,
Offspring of the Virgin's womb:
Veiled in flesh the Godhead see;
Hail th'Incarnate Deity,
Pleased as man with men to dwell,
Jesus, our Emmanuel.

Hail the heaven-born Prince of Peace!
Hail the Sun of Righteousness!
Light and life to all He brings,
Risen with healing in His wings.
Mild He lays His glory by,
Born that man no more may die,
Born to raise the sons of earth,
Born to give them second birth.

Refrain:

Hark! the herald angels sing,
"Glory to the new-born King."

Charles Wesley, alt. (1707-1788)

Hark, the Herald Angels Sing

[*Crusader Hymns*, No. 258]

A Hymn Story by Cliff Barrows

Some people become very disturbed when a publisher changes the words of an old hymn. Of course, this is not legally possible while a copyright is in force, and great caution must be exercised in "editing" a very old hymn that is now public property. A poet must be granted some rights with his own creation.

However, an author often makes alterations himself, even after his work has appeared in print. The first line of this Christmas hymn, as originally published in 1739, was "Hark, how all the welkin rings, Glory to the King of Kings!" Fourteen years later, author Charles Wesley changed those words to "Hark! the herald angels sing, Glory to the newborn King." During the ensuing decades there were many changes; some stanzas were dropped and others were rearranged. The hymn as we know it appeared in the *New Version* of the Tate and Brady Psalter in 1782, while Wesley was still living.

[Read or sing stanza 1.]

"Welkin" is an archaic word for "heavens" or "sky," and so we see that Wesley begins his hymn with the song of the angels on the first Christmas morning. "Glory to God in the highest heaven . . . and peace on earth, for all those pleasing Him" (Luke 2:14, *Living Gospels*). As we sing these deeply meaningful phrases, it soon becomes clear that this is something more than a simple Christmas carol. The phrase "God and sinners reconciled" reminds us that Christ came, not to enforce political amity, but to bring peace between God and man. The Christmas story is told concisely in II Corinthians 5:19 *(New English Bible):* "God was in Christ reconciling the world to himself." Of course this involves a change in us. As Romans 5:1 *(Living Letters)* says, "Since we have been made right in God's sight by faith in His promises, we can have real peace with Him because of what Jesus Christ our Lord has done for us." This is the peace promised by the angels on Christmas morning!

[Read or sing stanza 2.]

Throughout the hymn Charles Wesley continues to probe the deep mystery of Christmas, the mystery we call the Incarnation. Christ—who is the eternal King of heaven, worshipped by angels and archangels—lays aside the glory which is properly His, and condescends to be born of a virgin in a dark, dirty stable. Philippians 2:6 *(Phillips)* puts it this way: "For He, who had always been God by nature, did not cling to his prerogatives as God's equal, but stripped himself of all privilege by consenting to be a slave by nature and being born as mortal man."

Of course, Jesus was still God, and He often displayed His divine power and personality. But most men did not recognize Him as God because His divinity was hidden (the hymn says "veiled") in human flesh. This is the Lord of heaven who was pleased to dwell as a man with ordinary men. This also explains one of His names, found in the Old Testament and quoted by the angel to Joseph, "Behold, a virgin shall be with child, and shall bring forth a son, and they shall call his name *Emmanuel*, which being interpreted is, *God with us*" (Matt. 1:23).
[Read or sing stanza 3.]

Finally, the hymn reminds us of two more of Christ's names, given by Hebrew prophets long before His birth. The great passage in Isaiah 9:6 foretells: "And his name shall be called Wonderful, Counsellor, The Mighty God, The everlasting Father, The *Prince of Peace.*" Malachi 4:2 speaks also of the coming of Christ, "But unto you that fear my name shall the *Sun of righteousness* arise with healing in his wings." Wesley adds his own commentary about this figure of Christ the Sun. The physical sun is not only our source of light; it is the origin of life itself. Without the sun, all plant life would die. Without vegetation, animal life could not subsist. In the same way, Jesus Christ is the source of our spiritual light and our spiritual life.

Yes, Jesus' birth holds many mysteries. He who is immortal was born a mortal in order that man might live eternally with Him. He was born once in order that we might be born again.

Many folk who join in singing the carols, sharing all the happy festivities of Christmas, are unwilling to think of Christ in this way. It has been said that as long as we can keep Jesus as a charming baby in a manger, He makes no demands upon our lives. But Jesus was *born to die!* He grew to manhood, lived a perfect life, and then died on the cross, and rose again, for our eternal salvation. This is the true Christ of Christmas, and we must acknowledge Him our Lord, if we are to celebrate this season properly.

index

church calendar index